Low Cost Marketing

.

ROS JAY

in the Institute
of Management
FOUNDATION
PITMAN
PUBLISHING

PITMAN PUBLISHING
128 Long Acre, London WC2E 9AN

A Division of Longman Group Limited

First published in Great Britain 1994

© Ros Jay 1994

British Library Cataloguing in Publication Data
A CIP catalogue record for this book can be obtained
from the British Library.

ISBN 0 273 60439 2

1 3 5 7 9 10 8 6 4 2

Photoset in Linotron Century Schoolbook by
Northern Phototypesetting Co. Ltd., Bolton
Printed and bound in Great Britain
by Bell and Bain Ltd., Glasgow

*The Publishers' policy is to use paper manufactured
from sustainable forests*

Low Cost
Marketing

Ealing Tertiary Colleg

Contents

■

vi

Acknowledgements

■

I am very grateful to the following people for their co-operation, contributions and advice: Julian Baker, David Bernstein, Richard Craze, Annie Fanning, Tom Maschler, Penny Nelson, Dick Tracey, Mike Warne and Martin Woods. Also, I would especially like to thank Tony Jay for acting as consultant editor.

Introduction

■

Losers set out to sell what they know they can make; winners set out to make what they know they can sell.

Marketing is not a branch of the business, marketing *is* the business. It tells us what goods to make, how many, and by what date; what services to provide, what prices to charge, what discounts to offer; where and when to advertise, what to say to our customers, and how to say it. It is the engine that drives all the other activities. It is the difference between success and failure.

An interesting set of statistics was published recently, from a study of new businesses that looked into how they were getting on three years after starting up. They found that 72% of them had gone out of business and 24% of them were surviving but not growing. That left only 4% of companies actually thriving and expanding, taking on staff and increasing business. And what single feature did all of these successful businesses share? Every one was led by a marketing person.

So, how do you define a marketing person? Well, it has very little to do with experience, more to do with the way you think and approach problems. It's hard to be precise, but you can spot certain unifying features:

- they always think they're missing something
- they can admit to mistakes
- they take advice willingly.

David Bernstein, the marketing guru, defined a marketing person by saying: 'Marketing people may enjoy playing Scrabble because they appreciate language, but they *win* because they know it's really a numbers game.' He goes on to explain, 'I had a partner who's become a successful restaurateur because his love of food illuminates but never dictates his business. He also always beats me at Scrabble.'

It's not surprising if the people who are good at marketing are expensive. The ones with wide knowledge, a depth of experience and refined skills are deservedly among the highest paid members of the business community. They are also, by definition, out of our range. So, how can we low cost marketeers possibly match them on our budget?

The first answer is that we can't, but then we don't have to. We don't need to master the whole range of skills; all we need is to meet the needs of our own particular enterprise. They may employ brilliant writers and the world's finest photographers, but decent English and clear pictures will do us fine. They may devise complicated questionnaires to ask a balanced sample of three thousand people, and use techniques like distribution theory, regression analysis and the coefficient of determination to pro- duce a customer product profile, but a dozen phone calls and a morning in a shop chatting to customers may tell us all we need to know.

What we do need, however, is to master the basic elements of marketing. We must understand what steps we have to take and what mistakes we have to avoid. At every stage, there are expensive options and a low cost alternative; if we understand the principles there are few dangers in taking the low cost route. The purpose of this book is to clarify the principles and offer a range of low cost techniques for applying them. So in a sense it is, first of all, a basic guide to marketing and, secondly, a guide to getting the best results for the lowest outlay.

Each chapter deals with a different branch of marketing – research, pricing, public relations, advertising and so on – but underlying them all are the four basic rules for successful marketing on a limited budget (they're pretty good rules for marketing on a large budget, too):

- think
- talk
- do it yourself
- keep it simple.

Think

Rule one is *think* – all the time and in a structured way. Keep collecting and examining information. Analyse results. Ask questions. Test the answers. It costs nothing and means everything. The image of marketing may be one of flamboyant creativity, all panache and pizazz, and certainly these elements have their place, but the reality is intellectual rigour. Successful marketing ideas come from good information that has been analysed intelligently.

Above all, think like a customer – or a potential customer. Preferably a slightly unsatisfied one. What features of your product or service could be improved? What is missing? It was a manufacturer of children's pushchairs who put himself in the customers' position and felt unhappy about the inconvenience of carrying the chair when it was folded. So he redesigned the handles as hooks, allowing the folded chair to be hung over the forearm and leave both hands free.

All of us have a dissatisfied customer inside, full of free ideas and criticisms; the trick is to tune into that voice and listen to every word it says. So take time to sit down with the facts and figures and think hard about what they're telling you (and what they're not telling you).

You will need to think in two ways: on your own and with other people, and that takes us neatly on to our second rule.

Talk

Thinking on your own gives depth; thinking with other people gives breadth. You need them both. So, arrange meetings – even if there are only two of you – that are not for sorting out problems or despatching routine business, but for thinking and talking; for making sense of information, exploring new directions, criticising existing practices, learning from past experiences. It's the best value for money you will ever get.

Talk to people other than colleagues, and ask questions. Information is the foundation of successful marketing. Chapter 2, Research, lists techniques that cost little or nothing, but information gathering goes on all the time, and talking is the cheapest way to gather it.

So talk to your customers, to your retailers, to the staff behind the counter or at the end of the telephone. Talk to those who don't use your product or service as well as those who do. Talk to other people in the business – exhibitions and trade fairs offer an especially rich information harvest. The information you get will have little statistical validity, but it is a priceless source of insight and ideas, and invaluable for confirming suspicions or testing hunches.

Do it yourself

Rule three of low cost marketing is *do it yourself*. Once you put your business into the hands of research, advertising, design or marketing agencies, the costs start to explode. Doing it yourself can save a fortune. It's surprising how much you can do in-house if you have to. Desktop publishing, telephone research and selling, field research, press releases, advertisement layouts, slide presentations – it's surprising how far you can get on energy, enterprise and a bit of free professional advice.

And economy isn't the only benefit; when you do it yourself, you start to learn very fast. You identify the areas where professional help would be worth the money. You find what's fairly quick and easy, and what's slow and difficult. This means that if and when you do hire professionals, you have a much clearer idea of what you're asking them to do, and of how to focus their talents and their expensive time on the key areas.

If you do decide to pay for help, it's far cheaper to use single, freelance professionals than large agencies. A good designer, copywriter or researcher will conspire with you to hold down all the contingent costs – printing for example – that an agency might include in its bill, and add its own mark-up to.

Keep it simple

Rule four is *keep it simple*. In fact most things begin simple, then you start to complicate them later. The result is price structures of unfathomable complexity, discount arrangements that defeat even your own sales staff, advertisements that cram six illustrations and eleven product features into a quarter-page, instruction booklets that you need a doctorate to follow, and questionnaires so lengthy and involved that the respondents can't make sense of the questions and the analysts can't make sense of their answers. Complexity is the enemy of economy. The secret is clarity of intention maintained ruthlessly to completion.

Think, talk, do it yourself and keep it simple. These rules may not be the whole of marketing, but they're the way to get results out of all proportion to your financial outlay. In fact, these four disciplines would do no harm at all to medium cost and high cost marketing; but for low cost marketing they are the keys to the kingdom.

1

Planning

Thought is free

Shakespeare, *The Tempest*, Act III Scene ii

Suppose you have something to sell that you think is a really promising idea. It doesn't matter if you're setting up a new business, marketing a new product, brand or service or relaunching an old product. The good news is that you have this wonderful product to market – but the bad news is that you have next to no money to do it with. So how are you going to set about it?

There is only one way. You use that priceless resource that comes absolutely free: your ability to think. Not abstract philosophical reflection, but hard, structured, purposeful thought. Hard, because it must be based on all the ideas you can think up and all the hard facts you can get hold of; structured, because you have to address a sequence of questions; and purposeful, because you have to end up with a coherent and affordable marketing plan.

And you have to do your thinking before you do anything else, for two reasons. First, because it is at the start of a project that you are most likely to go wrong – because you have the least information and experience – and second, because the earlier you make a mistake the harder and more expensive it is to recover from it later.

Stage 1: forming the idea

Let's imagine that a friend of yours has pulled off a bit of a coup. The factory where he works was re-equipping with new, automated machine tools, and he picked up a set of the old ones for almost nothing. What's more, he's got quite a large shed at the back of his house and he's a skilled operator. He could start making things and selling them. But what things? The two of you talked about, it but nothing realistic cropped up.

Then, at the weekend, you were gardening. You weren't thinking about Pete's mini-factory, you were too busy struggling with the climbing roses and the rotten wooden posts and trellises they were coming away from. There must be a better way of training climbers, you were thinking. And suddenly, it clicked. Metal climbing frames! Pete's machines would be ideal for cutting, bending and shaping the sort of material you'd need.

The next day you meet up with Pete. He thinks it's a terrific idea. You both get really excited. You could leave work and start up on your own. Ideas fall over each other. Standard frames, wall frames, fencing frames, edging frames. Topiary-style frames in bird and animal shapes. Frames in the shape of every letter of the alphabet. Heavy duty and lightweight frames. And the market! Gardeners, market gardeners, municipal parks, industrial land-scaping. Bespoke contracts for business parks. Consultancy. A planting and maintenance division for corporate customers. Exports to Europe and America ... the possibilities are boundless.

And that is the heart of the problem. The possibilities are indeed boundless, but if you pursue them all at once, you'll find yourself needing a warehouse full of different products, a corporate sales force, a retail sales force, a direct mail operation, and about a dozen separate advertising media. It is a safe bet that you'll go bust in the time it takes to say 'cash flow forecast'.

If you had a fortune to spend you could rent a suite of offices, recruit a lot of staff, take on expensive marketing consultants, appoint a top advertising agency, rent a few factories, and try a whole range of approaches. But you haven't got a fortune. There's just you and Pete and a few thousand pounds of savings you're prepared to risk.

So how do you set about thinking your way towards a marketing plan? The answer is that you have already started. That excited conversation you had with Pete was stage one – a product brainstorming session. Perhaps you noted down the ideas at the time. If not, note them down now. Then get together with Pete again, and perhaps one or two friends – especially if they know about gardening, retailing or metal fabrication – and think up all the product ideas you can.

The rules for successful brainstorming are few but strict:

- every idea must be written down
- no adverse comments or criticism are allowed
- don't stick rigidly to a tight agenda – whoever chairs the session should only intervene if the group gets right off the subject.

An hour and a half is usually the maximum time you should spend brainstorming, with about an hour being the optimum length of time. At the end of it you should have a mass of suggestions, some of them pretty silly, and none of them in any particular order.

3

Stage 2: the cold light of day

After the euphoria of the brainstorming session has died down, you meet again and discuss the list of ideas. First of all you eliminate: cross out the ones you know are out of the question, at least for the early stages of the project. If you have a doubt, give the idea the benefit of it.

Then grade the ideas, starting with the most promising, but remember that at this stage the grading is very tentative, so don't agonise too much over the choice.

Stage 3: asking the questions

Right. So now you have some really promising products, but not much of an idea as to which ones are going to work. That takes you to stage three. Stage three is hard work. It is where you list, as systematically as you can, all the questions you need to answer to help you find exactly the right product or service, and set about marketing it in the right way.

The questions will fall under three headings:

1 questions about the customer
2 questions about the product or service
3 questions about the business.

Or to put it another way, who are your customers, what are you offering them, and will it make a profit? Some questions you will be able to answer straight away. Others will expose the need for more information. As you go through, make a list of all the missing facts.

THE CUSTOMER

Let's say that the products at the top of your list are decorative fencing and free-standing frames in original shapes. There are certain questions you must try to answer about the customers for these products. In fact, they are the questions everyone has to answer, whatever they are marketing. This applies just as much if you are marketing a new product or service for an established company.

You never find the final answer – you may not end up with much more than a guess – but you have to ask the questions nevertheless and produce the best answers you can.

Who are the customers?

Are they old or young? Private individuals or other businesses? Urban, suburban or rural? North or South? Wealthy, middling or hard up? Male or female? Is the person who forks out the cash actually the one who makes the decision?

What price will they pay?

How much are they paying at the moment for similar products? Would they pay more for something better? Would they buy a lot more if it was a lot cheaper?

What are they using at the moment?

Or, to put it another way, who are your principal competitors? What quantities do they buy from each one? With what frequency?

What are the trends?

It is obviously important to know what your potential customers are buying now, but it is also necessary to find out if this represents a rise or fall over the past few years. Not just for the product or service – fencing and so on – but also for the whole market; is the national annual spend on gardeners' hardware going up or down?

What features do they go for?

Are they price-conscious? Is it strength and durability that come first? Is it a status display purchase – something bought with a view to impressing friends, neighbours or colleagues? Obviously this will vary from customer to customer, but the answers will help give you a clearer picture of the market as a whole.

How will they find out about it?

Will they just see it in a shop or a garden centre? Will we have to advertise? Can we place it as a news item in gardening magazines? Should we take a stand at an exhibition? Could we get an exhibiting rose grower to use our frames for nothing and give out our leaflet?

Where will they buy it?

From garden centres? DIY stores? Hardware shops? By mail order? By cutting out a coupon from newspapers or magazines? From someone else's catalogue?

Why should they choose our product or service rather than someone else's?

What has it got that none of the others can offer – what is its USP (Unique Selling Proposition)? This can be highest quality, lowest price, best design, fastest delivery, strongest construction or some other unique feature. Or it could be a value trade-off; for example, the most robust frame in its price range.

Obviously you will not be able to answer all these questions completely or even, in many cases, satisfactorily. What's more you could spend that fortune you have not got in the attempt. In Chapter 2, Research, we examine the cheap ways of getting useful answers. The important point to note at this stage, however, is that you must keep a very open mind about the product or service.

As you collect more and more market information, some of the ideas that were at the top of your list may start to look doubtful and drop down the list, while some of the ones that were lower down may start to look rather more promising.

THE PRODUCT OR SERVICE

Exactly which products or services you are going to market is one of the fundamental decisions you will have to make, and the 'customer' questions are designed to help you get it right.

Actually making the product is a manufacturing and not a marketing problem; nevertheless it has a marketing dimension, and there are questions here, too, that you need to answer – or at least ask – at a very early stage.

How will it look?

Packaging and presentation are marketing decisions, but they belong at the product design stage. Most products involve a number of arbitrary decisions – colour is one of the most obvious – that can make the product easier or harder to sell. For example, extra-wide tyres make a cheap car look powerful and may justify adding more to the price than the extra cost of fitting them.

6

Who will supply the materials?

This also has an impact on marketing. Can you get supplies of the quality you need, or in the colours the customers will want? Is the only supplier at the other end of the country? Can they supply you as fast as you want to supply your customers? Will the cost of supplies push the price up above what your customers want to pay?

How will it transport?

This is not a problem with ballpoint pens, say, but with larger products it can be significant. One of the most successful marketing ideas IKEA, the Scandinavian furniture megastore, had was to design every possible piece of furniture so that it could be carried away by the customer in a flat-pack box. Perhaps we should design our frames for flat-pack transportation? Perhaps not; but it is a marketing decision that needs to be made at the product design stage. Factors such as weight and shape can create distribution problems, as well as point-of-sale display problems.

Will it create problems for the customer?

It is all too easy to design irritation into a product without realising it. Have you ever spent half a day putting together a self-assembly product that you thought would only take 20 minutes? If customers have to assemble it, then ease of assembly has to be part of the design specification – ease for people with no eye for that kind of thing, not just for qualified engineers. You can also design into the product problems the customer will encounter in operating it, maintaining it and repairing it; or you can design them out. But only at the design stage.

How easily can we increase volume?

Suppose your product is a runaway success. Pete's shed and his set of tools won't be enough. You will have to expand. This may mean buying new tools, which at this stage you probably cannot afford. Or you may have to subcontract the work. That's fine if you took it into account when you costed the production, but if all your costs are based on Pete's time and Pete's tools, the costs of subcontracting may take all your profits if you try to expand production.

Will it need explaining?

If assembly, operation, maintenance and repair are not completely straightforward, you may have to include explanatory leaflets, booklets or manuals with the product. This is not a problem if you have planned for it from the start, but if you suddenly discover you have to do it when you are already in production, it can cause acute pain in the cash flow and profit region.

THE BUSINESS

The business questions are chiefly but not exclusively financial, and are dealt with in Chapter 3, Pricing. You can easily produce a terrific product, which sells like hot cakes, and end up in the bankruptcy court. A central part of marketing, arguably its very foundation, is ensuring that you end up with a profit, not a loss. Not only that, but costing obviously affects price, and the price you charge for a product is inextricably bound up with how you market it. This means you cannot leave the business questions until later; their answers must be built into the initial plan.

So that's stage three. It won't be that straightforward because as you think about questions in, say, the business sections, it will stimulate new questions about the customer and the product. But by the end of it you should have a list of facts you need to know. Some will be of only moderate significance, some will be important, and some will be central to the success of the whole enterprise. So stage four is collecting the facts.

8

Stage 4: collecting the facts

If you had money to burn, you could hire a market research agency to do this for you. But you haven't, so you will have to use alternatives. That is what Chapter 2, Research, is all about. You never get all the information you want; you will have to supplement it with rough estimates, intelligent guesses and a feel for the business and the customer.

If time is short (and however much time you have it is never enough) it is usually a good idea to adopt the Bragg strategy. Sir Lawrence Bragg was a brilliant research scientist. Not only did he win the Nobel Prize in 1916 for his work on X-ray crystallography, he was also leader of the team at the Cavendish Laboratory in Cambridge that cracked the genetic coding of DNA.

One of the reasons for Bragg's success was his research strategy: he didn't always start with the most promising line of inquiry. Sometimes, the most promising line will take a long time before it delivers any useful results, and if they turn out to be negative after all, the time has been wasted. Bragg looked for other promising lines that offered quick results. This meant that if the results were negative, he could eliminate them very rapidly – or move on fast if the results were positive.

9

Whether you are conducting scientific research or market research, this is a sensible time-saving (and therefore money-saving) approach to take. So as you go through the list of facts to collect and lines of inquiry to pursue, it is worth grading them not only by importance but also by the time and expense you will have to invest before they yield useful information. So the first research to do is the research that will give you answers quickly and cheaply, even if the answer it gives you is 'don't bother with this at the moment'. Save the expensive, complicated research until you are sure you can't get the answers you need without it. Then, when you've done the best you can, you are in a position to make the first important decisions:

- what product(s) or service(s) to sell
- at what price

- what annual sales volume you are aiming for.

Stage 5: brainstorming

When you have determined those things, you are ready for stage five, which is another brainstorming session. Same rules, but this time it's not a product but a marketing brainstorm: all the ideas you can think of for places where you can sell the product or service, people or organisations you can sell it to, channels of communication with them, ways of persuading them they want to buy it. Then, as before, you wait and take a cool look at the ideas and pick the most promising ones.

Stage 6: SWOT analysis

You are now almost ready to draw up the marketing plan. This is the time to take a couple of paces backwards and look at your whole operation – to be, as it were, your own management consultant. You don't have to follow a formula, but SWOT – the acronym for Strengths, Weaknesses, Opportunities, Threats – provides as good a structure as any, and will sharpen your mental focus when you plan your strategy.

STRENGTHS

If you work for a large organisation, these could include massive financial muscle, an international sales force, a worldwide reputation, factories spread across the globe, a string of valuable patents and copyrights, and a vast research laboratory. You and Pete are not in that league. Well, not yet anyway. But you have other strengths:

- you have low costs and low overheads
- you are flexible – you can change product design and marketing tactics far more quickly than a corporate megamonster can
- you can get quick decisions – there's no corporate hierarchy in the way, and you don't have to spend half your time at inter-

departmental meetings

- you can get information quickly to all branches of the organisation, so long as you and Pete stay on speaking terms
- you are speaking directly to your customers instead of communicating with them via sales departments and retail staff
- you are your own best salesperson – you are more motivated than the average salesperson because you are selling your own idea, your own product.

As you look at your strengths it becomes clear that your big advantage is that you can change very fast – you can always be ahead of the game. But only if flexibility, regular customer research and frequent reviews of product design and marketing tactics are built into your marketing philosophy.

WEAKNESSES

Despite your strengths, you do have areas of weakness:

- you're short of cash, which means, as we said at the start, that you have to make up for it by thinking harder. This can be a positive advantage: you get far better results by thinking your way through problems than by buying your way out of them. But it also means that you can have problems not only if your fencing doesn't sell, but also if it sells too well and you want to expand quickly.
- you will, at least to start with, find it hard to get credit
- you have no established brand name to build on
- you may also be at the mercy of the seasons; people don't do much gardening in the winter
- another weakness is overdependence, whether on a single customer, a single supplier or key staff: what happens if Pete walks under a bus? (Yes, you can take out key personnel insurance, if you can afford it.)

Larger companies often have weaknesses in the same areas where smaller companies have strengths:

- they are often less adaptable
- their internal communications are more unwieldy
- it's harder to achieve a personal rapport with the customers.

A limited product range can be a weakness, or a product line which is very susceptible to a bad economic climate, such as fitted kitchens (though sales of chocolate bars and baked beans increase during a recession; your product's response to a weak economy could be a strength). Geographical location could also be a weakness (high distribution costs) or a strength (lower rates of pay).

Every company is different and unique, so a comprehensive list is impossible. But if you can identify your weaknesses fully and honestly, it will guide you in the formation of your marketing strategy.

OPPORTUNITIES

While strengths and weaknesses are an integral part of your company's make-up (though not necessarily unchangeable), opportunities and threats come from the outside. They can come from customers, suppliers, competitors, the media, government policy, new regulations – but always from outside.

- Are there events coming up that would give you a showcase?
- Are there new or proposed laws or regulations that will help the sales of metal rather than wood?
- Are there new guidelines on the screening of eyesores that will open the way for fencing?
- Are there government grants for small businesses or for help with exports?
- Is there help from the EC in finding European partners or distributors?

An established business should be constantly on the lookout for new opportunities; it's a good idea to arrange a regular session, say once every month or two, to focus on them. Perhaps a new raw material is available that will cut production costs dramatically, or a competitor has gone bust, leaving lots of customers looking for a new supplier. You might hit on these by chance, but a structured and focused spell of thinking purely about opportunities will throw up a lot more.

THREATS

- How vulnerable are you to competition? Could a rival producer make a big price cut or launch an expensive advertising campaign or sales drive?
- Are there new laws in the offing that could force you to increase costs for reasons of safety or hygiene?
- Could a single legal action for negligence cripple you?
- Would you be seriously hit by a big rise in interest rates?
- What if a big customer went bust owing you a lot of money?
- What if a key supplier went out of business?
- Might any key staff leave to work for a competitor?

13

Thinking about all these dangers in advance may suggest simple and cheap ways of forestalling them. Obviously a complete list is impossible, but these examples may give you an idea of the areas you should be exploring before you sit down and draw up your marketing plan.

Once you've identified your strengths, weaknesses, opportunities and threats, you need to do something about them. For each point you've noted down, ask yourself two questions. First, why is it a strength/weakness/opportunity/threat? It's easy to put points under the wrong heading; asking this question will ensure that you have put them in the right place. If you haven't, you won't be able to answer the second question, which is: how can we exploit this strength/opportunity, or eliminate this weakness/threat? If you don't answer this question, you have achieved nothing by doing the analysis – this is the question that spurs you into action to change and improve things.

And now, finally, you are ready for stage seven.

Stage 7: the marketing plan

There is no single correct format for a marketing plan. Some of them are extremely long and complicated, but you will want to keep yours as short and simple as possible. But whatever the format, there are five elements every marketing plan has to include.

1 THE KEY FACTS ABOUT THE PRODUCT, SERVICE OR RANGE

Of course you know these. So does Pete. But even between the two of you there may be differences you hadn't identified. Only by writing the facts down will you sort them out. And you will want a clear, full and accurate description of the product to show other people. This section should include the price or price range.

2 THE KEY FACTS ABOUT THE CUSTOMERS

If you are selling to separate markets – home gardeners and public authorities for example – they will, of course, have to be treated separately. This section will include:

- who they are
- what they spend at the moment
- what they want
- how you will tell them about the product
- where they will buy it.

3 THE SALES FORECAST

This may be largely guesswork, but 'forecast' sounds better. It will be based on the break-even figure – since a forecast of less than break-even is a proposal for commercial hara-kiri – but obviously it must be for more. It should be phased, week by week or month by month, to take account of factors like a slower initial selling rate and seasonal buying patterns. It will also be the basis of your production schedule.

4 OPPORTUNITIES AND THREATS

List the chief opportunities you identified in Stage 6, the SWOT analysis, and how you plan to capitalise on them. For example, there may be new funding available from the EC that you intend to put in an application for. Likewise, list the main threats and briefly how you plan to prepare for them or counter them.

5 THE MARKETING STRATEGY

This will consist of many ingredients. Always try to quantify them if you can. For instance:

- telephone selling – how many connected calls per day?
- mailshots – to how many people? How frequently? Where will the mailing lists come from? Who will create the literature?
- advertising – in which media? How often? Who will create the material?
- exhibitions – which ones? Who builds the stand? Who staffs it?
- sales visits – how many per week?
- discounts – what percentage? To whom? Will they increase according to the quantity ordered?
- payment terms – cash on the nail? 15 days' credit? 30 days? 90? Sale or return?
- delivery – what method of transport? Who pays?
- after-sales service, repairs, and so on – how will they be advertised? Who undertakes them? How will they be paid for? Do we give guarantees?

This list is not meant to be exclusive. You will have other ideas as well, but whatever you decide on will have budget and time implications, so everything you include in the plan must be costed and time-scheduled. Otherwise you will find you have to be 200 miles from base at a trade show for the week in which you have to finalise all the copy for your main mailshot of the year.

15

MARKETING PLAN CHECKLIST

1 The product or service
- description
- price or price range

2 The customers
- profile of existing customers
- profile of future customers
- method of advertising/publicising product or service
- outlets

3 Sales forecast

4 Opportunities

5 Threats

6 Marketing strategy

Obviously the marketing plan does not have the immutable authority of the Ten Commandments. Nothing is set in stone. Quite the reverse; every day of trading brings in new information, and some of it will mean revising the plan. So build review sessions into the schedule. But unless you have a plan there is nothing to review or revise.

By the time you have finished stage seven you will have a marketing plan, a marketing schedule and a marketing budget; the budget should show not only how much will have to be spent, but also when. It has cost you a lot of thought and work, but virtually no money, and put you in a strong position – stronger than a lot of other organisations that have money to spend but can't spare enough time to think. It doesn't guarantee success because nothing does that, but it cuts out a whole lot of mistakes that guarantee failure.

And that's really it. But there is one last precaution that's worth taking. Show the finished plan to a colleague or friend with a good critical mind and go through it with them to see if they can spot any flaws. It must be someone who hasn't been involved in the project. They may come up with some really good questions. Even if they don't, their comments may alert you to potential dangers or possible improvements. And then, after a final review session, you are ready to go.

Research

Talk is cheap

Market research serves four vital functions:

1 to monitor the changes in how your customers see you and what they want from you
2 to explore the reasons behind a problem
3 to identify new markets for your products or services
4 to identify new products or services for your market.

The more tightly you target your market, the more efficiently you will be spending your money. So if you haven't much money to start with, market research is vital – and the more thorough it is the better.

The problem is that you can get stuck in a catch-22: you need to do the research to save money, but the research itself costs money. So we're back to rule three of low cost marketing: *do it yourself*.

A lot of people go weak at the knees at the prospect of doing their own research. They avoid the mere thought of it, for the perfectly good reason that they haven't the first idea how to go about it. This chapter is for people who can't afford an alternative. Chapter 1 identified what we need to know; now let's look at the practical side of how we find it out:

- where to find ready-made information

- how to gather new information

- how to make sense of the results.

Keep asking what your customers want

Whether you are starting up a new business or running a long established one, you are going to have to research your market. In some ways it's easier if the company is new – you can see that it needs doing, and you know which questions need answering. If your business has been going a long time, it's easy to think you know the answers already. But it's not as simple as that. The market is constantly changing, and you need to research that change to make sure you develop alongside it.

The real difference between marketing and non-marketing companies is the ability to change. Customers will always leave – companies go bust, people move out of the area, they prefer your competitors, they haven't got time for that hobby any more – so you need to recruit new customers all the time simply to stand still. You need to work even harder if you want to grow. And the market's always changing; what's right today will be wrong tomorrow. So you need to keep researching it.

Once you get used to researching what your customers want, you may discover all sorts of opportunities. One insurance consultant, for example, discovered that his clients really wanted to be able to sort out their insurance needs faster and more simply. So he set up a new company selling life and health insurance, but he computerised all the data so that anyone could operate it. He now offers insurance over the telephone, the turnaround time is faster for each customer and the administration has been cut down. He's doing a roaring trade – because he listened to his customers.

KNOW WHEN TO STOP

The longer you spend doing your research, the more accurate it will be. Really expensive research can tell you accurately (within about 1.5%) how many people will walk past your new shop each week, for example. But do you really need to be that precise? Of course in an ideal world it would be great. But if all you need to know is that at least 100 people will visit, don't spend your precious money on finding out any more than that.

Using a market research agency

Before we get down to the nitty-gritty of DIY market research, it's worth mentioning that it can occasionally be more sensible to use a specialist. For example:

- the agency (or freelance) may specialise in an industry that you don't know enough about to do the research yourself
- you may lack certain necessary skills – foreign languages, for example, or a bent for statistical analysis
- it is easier for an outsider to be critical of your company's internal practices. So if you think the research might need to highlight any in-house deficiency, it can be better not to do it yourself
- quantitative research (asking hundreds or thousands of people exactly the same questions) may be more cost effective if you use an agency.

The best approach is to work out the cost of doing the research yourself (including the cost of your time, of course), and then compare the figure with quotes from market research agencies. To reduce the cost, you could ask an agency to do only part of the work for you – just collect the information, say, or only process information you've collected.

If you decide to use an agency, remember that you're paying for their overheads as well as their research. It might be better to find a single freelance researcher, just as you can often get a building job done much more cheaply by directly employing the plumber, the electrician and the carpenter than by using a building firm.

But be careful; you have to be very clear about what you want, and know how to tell if it's being done properly or not. That's why doing it yourself, at least occasionally, or at the start, is such a good discipline – it makes you much better at getting value for money when you use professionals.

If you do want to use an agency or a freelance, the Market Research Society (see Useful Addresses at the end of this book) produces an annual directory called *Organisations and Individuals Providing Market Research Services*, which is available for the cost of the postage.

OMNIBUS RESEARCH

If you are lucky enough to have a modest budget available, there is one form of low cost agency research that is worth mentioning: omnibus research. Research companies that offer this service interview a large number of people, say a couple of thousand, and ask them a large number of questions. You pay for just one or two of these questions to be yours, while other companies are filing other questions. This works out relatively cheaply as you are sharing the questionnaire with a lot of other companies.

Desk research   21

As we saw in Chapter 1, a large part of planning involves asking questions, about your customers, your suppliers, your competitors and so on. Once you have drawn up your list of questions, you need to divide them into two categories:

- questions you can look up the answers to
- questions you will have to find the answers to by talking to people.

The first category is known as desk research. You can find the answers to plenty of questions about your industry, your type of product, your potential suppliers and your kind of customers this way. There is plenty of published information that tells you about industry trends, typical customer profiles for certain products, current prices, advertising costs (and magazine readership), suppliers, lists of possible outlets and so on. But before you head off to camp out at your local library for a week, have another thinking session first.

THINK

Rule one of low cost marketing: *think*. Do you remember being five years old? At that age, we want to learn as much as we can about everything around us – people, places, technology – so we keep asking questions. We drive our parents mad with interminable questions. Why do bubbles come up when you put an empty milk bottle under water? That's the air inside the bottle escaping. Why does it need to escape? Because it's lighter than the water so it wants to float on it. Why are the bubbles round and not square? . . .

So now you want to know everything about your market – the customers, the competition, the price you can charge and so on. So keep asking yourself questions. Why do people grow climbing plants on frames? To add shape to their gardens. What shapes do they want to add? They want to add height. How much height? Usually more than a tall herbaceous plant and less than a small tree – about four to eight feet. Right – so that's probably the best height for the free-standing frames. Now you've thought your way through a large chunk of the question 'how tall should the frames be?' and you just need to do a little more research to back it up.

Marketing really isn't about flair and panache. It's actually about hard, clear thinking. Perhaps the easiest way to demonstrate this is to give you three real examples of smart thinking.

The dentist

Murray Hawkins is a qualified dentist. He wanted to move to the South West of England and set up his own practice. Where should he go? Where there were likely to be a lot of people needing dental treatment. Where would that be? Wherever the ratio of dentists to people was lowest. How would he know where that was?

He looked up the populations of every main town in the South West. Then he looked up the number of dentists in each of them. He discovered that Gillingham had the lowest ratio, so he decided to move there. But now he wanted to know whereabouts in

Gillingham to be. So he asked another question: 'What am I really best at?' The answer was that he was terrific with kids – they often actually enjoyed a trip to the dentist. He made sure there was plenty for them to play with, pictures painted on the ceiling and so on. So where are the kids? At school.

He set up the Murray Hawkins Dental Practice opposite the gates of one of the biggest schools in Gillingham, where parents could meet the kids from school and take them to the dentist on the way home. Yes, it worked a treat.

The hotelier

This particular hotelier wanted to advertise the fact that his hotel grounds had a river frontage with fishing rights. But advertising in the *Angling Times* cost more than he wanted to spend. And it was full of other hotels advertising exactly the same thing. So he asked a question: who goes fishing? He did some research and discovered that 70% of GPs go fishing. How could he reach this market? He took a stand at an exhibition of supplies and equipment for doctors. This was much cheaper than a stand at an exhibition for anglers, and his was the only hotel there. A large proportion of his customers nowadays are doctors.

23

The District Council

The Tourism and Marketing department of South Somerset District Council wanted to promote holidays that would encourage nice, quiet tourists who could be accommodated in small hotels and guest houses. They didn't want to encourage large, rowdy groups, and they don't have any huge hotels in South Somerset. What groups of tourists would be small, quiet and appreciate the local scenery? They came up with several answers, including cyclists. Their district covers much of the famous, flat Somerset Levels – a beautiful area for easy cycling – so they decided to promote cycling holidays. They couldn't afford a huge advertising campaign, and they needed to target their market very precisely.

The next question was: who would want to go cycling on the Somerset Levels? People who like to cycle in flat areas. Who are they? The people who cycle in other flat areas. What other flat areas are there? One of the most notoriously flat places is Holland. The District Council couldn't afford to advertise in lots of foreign language publications, but the Dutch speak excellent English, and tend to like England. Not only that, but they take more holidays abroad per capita than any other European nation. And the Somerset 'rhynes' are similar to the dykes of Holland.

So the District Council advertised their cycling routes and cycling holidays in Holland, through cycling clubs and exhibitions. It was a huge success; you see more Dutch people in Somerset these days than you ever used to.

These examples should have given you an idea of the kinds of questions to ask yourself, and the sort of thinking to do. And you can see that these people saved themselves a lot of time by thinking first, before they started their research proper. Once you've thought through this process on your own, do it again with colleagues or friends. It's well worth it. Thinking alone is often better for focusing on a question or problem and analysing it in depth. Thinking in groups is less likely to achieve this, but it is usually the better way of sparking off lateral thought – sideways jumps of logic – and generating new ideas.

WHERE TO LOOK FOR INFORMATION

Now you know precisely which questions you want to answer, there are several places you can go, such as:

- libraries
- trade associations and regulatory bodies
- government departments
- local enterprise agencies
- trade press.

Libraries

You may have a large local library that gives you access to all the information you want. But if you need to go further afield, there are several good business libraries around the country (ask your local library where the nearest one is). You can usually borrow any book you want through the interlibrary lending scheme, which your library should also be able to give you details about. There is also a Science Reference Library in London, which is invaluable for information about patents, trademarks, and science and technology.

There are several publications that are likely to be useful and which a good library will have:

■ *Kompass* is a directory of British companies, listed by industry, product, name and location

■ *Directory of British Associations* lists associations and societies that may well be able to give you information you need

■ *Municipal Year Book* is a directory of local authorities and includes contact names

■ *The Source Book* gives you marketing information organised by services and industry sectors; it will also provide you with information about directories, trade associations, statistics and so on

■ *Marketsearch* publishes about 20 000 market research reports covering markets around the world

■ *BRAD (British Rate and Data)* is a listing of every newspaper and magazine in Britain and gives distribution figures, advertising rates and so on, for trade publications, national papers and local freesheets

■ *Yellow Pages*: many libraries stock a complete set, covering the whole country.

This is only a selection of the most commonly used business source books, and you probably won't want to use all of these, but it gives you an idea of the type and range of information you can get from the library. A large library will also provide access to a number of

25

on-line database services. These carry all sorts of information, such as financial data, key personnel, sales figures and so on for British or overseas companies, overseas sales leads, grants and loans or information about specific industries. Many smaller libraries also subscribe to some of these, and will carry out a search (for a price).

Trade associations and regulatory bodies

Many of these organisations publish annual reports, surveys and so on giving details of the industry. They will often give you this information free, but they may charge a fee. The same goes for many regulatory bodies, such as the Chartered Institutes, Fimbra, the Law Society and so on. They should be listed in the *Directory of British Associations.*

Government departments

The Government produces a wealth of information that you may find helpful. You can get hold of a listing of their publications from the Central Statistical Office. These include social and economic trends, retail price indices, census reports, overseas trade statistics and many more. Companies House can give you financial information on companies free at their London office or for a nominal fee by post from their Cardiff office.

The Department of Trade and Industry has regional centres around the country, which are often very helpful with trade and export advice and help for new businesses through their Enterprise Initiative.

Local enterprise agencies

These agencies can give lots of advice, often completely free, to new and established businesses. They all offer slightly different services, but most will give free information and advice on exporting, marketing, and grants and loans. Some also subscribe to on-line databases of information about British companies,

EC legislation and other useful topics. You can get details of your local enterprise agency through Business in the Community (see Useful Addresses at the end of this book).

Trade press

Somewhere in the region of 7500 newspapers, magazines and periodicals are published every year in this country. The specialist magazines for various trades are all listed in *BRAD* (a copy of which should be held at your nearest main library). For example, it lists a handful of specialist publications for garden centres, and several for landscapers and garden designers.

Get hold of copies of the leading trade publications – even pay for them if you must – but the chances are that the advertising managers will send them free, along with an advertising rate card. The editors of these publications know their industries inside out, and if you are really stuck on a vital question of research, they may be able to give you the answer, if you ask nicely. They're busy people, though, and you won't get far if you ring them up with long lists of queries.

YOUR OWN RECORDS

If you've been in business for any length of time, your own customer records should be one of the best sources of information you will ever get your hands on. What have they bought before? How price sensitive are they (how many customers did you lose last time you put your prices up)? Unless you are branching into a totally new field with no customer overlap at all, this information is invaluable. What's more, it's free – and not available to your competitors.

It's also really hard information. You can ask people what they think they might like and how much they might be prepared to spend, but how far will you be able to believe the answer? It's quite another matter if you have concrete evidence that they did buy it, and how much they forked out for it. (Chapter 10 looks at what customer records you need to keep.)

554 *Business & Professional Publications* — **GARDEN SUPPLIES, EQUIPMENT AND CENTRES**

cols 233. 6 cols 280. Screen: mono and 2 colour 48, full colour 60. Screen: mono 48 60, colour 60. Litho. Mono positives right reading emulsion side down, colour positives right reading emulsion side down

Deadlines Copy 2nd Friday of the month preceding publication date. Cancellation 42 days preceding publication date

Advertisement — Supplementary statement by publisher

Since its launch in October 1984, **KBBReview** has won the hearts and minds of the industry it serves.

KBBReview is also the market's preferred advertising choice by a mile showing the strength of our commitment to editorial quality and excellence.

In current market conditions, the accuracy and comprehensiveness of circulations are now more important than ever. We have been building, strengthening and re-registering our cirulation.

KBBReview is the only magazine in the market always published every month and on time. **KBBReview's** circulation is over 99% requesting at 12,000 plus per month.

Call John Shanahan - 0895 677677 for the latest information

KITCHEN, BEDROOM & BATHROOM REVIEW PRODUCT CARDS

Publisher DMG Home Interest Magazines Ltd. Times House, Station Approach, Ruislip, Middlesex, HA4 8NB. Tel 0895 677677. Fax 0895 676027

Contacts Editor Sarah Carlile, Publishing & Exhibition Director Jette Gorvin, Advertisement Manager John Shanahan, Advertisement Production Sally Miller, Publisher Michael Franks

Advertisement Sales Provincial. DMG Home Interest Magazines Ltd. The Hollies, 53 Brierly Green, Buxworth, Stockport, Cheshire SK12 7NL. Tel 0663 751937

Contacts Provincial Office Beverley Burkett

Supplement to **Kitchen Bedroom & Bathroom Review**

Frequency Monthly

Circulation Bound-in. See **Kitchen Bedroom & Bathroom Review**

Rates Effective 1 January 1994

Mono Rates Mono: Card rop £400.00, series 3 £380.00, 6 £360.00, 12 £340.00

Production Specifications Advertisement size 130 × 130 inc product illustration and up to 120 words text

PINE NEWS INTERNATIONAL

Est 1986

Publisher Nigel Gearing Ltd, 4 Red Barn Mews, High Street, Battle, East Sussex, TN33 0AG

Contacts Publisher Nigel Gearing, Journal Manager Peter Wickenden, Editor John Legg, Production Tony Kilby, Dennis Flowers

Editorial Tel 0424 775305. Fax 0424 774321

Advertisement Sales Tel 0424 774988 774982. Fax 0424 774321

Frequency Monthly

Price Single copy free Per year £25

Editorial Profile Trade news, reproduction pine, antique pine, timber talk, countrystyle accessories, technical talk. Down to earth style, favours small, punchy news articles

Circulation Uncertified

Target Readership Subscribed readers in retail, contract furnishing, distributors, designers, manufacturers, government buying agencies and the general manufacturers of accessories, subscribed to worldwide on all aspects of the pine industry

Rates Received 25 January 1993 Agency Commission 10%

Standard Rates

mono page £574.00

Mono Rates Mono: Page rop £574.00. Half rop £290.00. Quarter rop £147.00. Eighth rop £74.00. Series discount 2 5%, 6 7.50%, 10 10%

Cover Rates earpiece £50.00

Colour Rates Full colour: Full page rop £1179.00. Half rop £758.00. Quarter rop £443.00. Eighth rop £222.00. 1 standard spot colour: rop 20% extra

Classified Rates Scc rop £3.50

Production Specifications Covers page size 390 × 285, type page size 375 × 285, half 375 × 140 or 185 × 285, quarter 185 × 140, eighth 90 × 140. Col width 44. No of cols 6. Screen: mono 40, colour 48. Colour: Web Heatset. Mono: Coldset. Mono: one-piece bromides. Colour: negative film, right-reading emulsion side up. Print Order 1 November 1993 edition 7,700 (Publisher's Statement)

Deadlines Copy 3 weeks preceding publication date. Cancellation 3 weeks preceding publication date

GARDEN SUPPLIES, EQUIPMENT AND CENTRES
(also see Horticultural)

Advertisement — Cross Listing

DIY WEEK

HARDWARE • HOUSEWARES • GARDEN • DIY

DIY WEEK

Incorporating Do It Yourself Retailing, The Ironmonger, Hardware Merchandiser, Domestic Electrical Appliances, Lighting, Ironmongery & Hardware, Hardware Trade Journal

Affiliations ABC BBP PPA

Publisher Benn Publications Ltd. Sovereign Way, Tonbridge, Kent TN9 1RW. Tel 0732 364422. Telex 95132 BENTON G. Fax 0732 361534

Advertisement Sales West Midlands. Benn Publications Ltd. Manor House, Manor Lane, Halesowen, West Midlands B62

Editorial Profile Business to business publication for the owners, operators and managers of garden centres. Articles cover all topics pertinent to running a modern and independent garden centre

Regular Features *(by BRAD Classification)* Environment & Conservation. Gardening & Plants. Pets. Sport Fencing. Conservation. Garden Supplies Equipment & centres

Special Features

1 May 1994	Merchandising to greater profits
1 June 1994	Retailing seeds and bulbs - avoid the pitfalls for better profits
1 July 1994	Garden centre design - what does the future hold in store? Lessons from around the world
1 August 1994	(August September) Glee and Autumn fair previews. Four Oaks preview
1 October 1994	PLan now for next year's bedding. Regional survey of how the 94 season went
1 November 1994	(November December) Garden Machinery - a growth area for garden centres

Circulation Uncertified

RES available

Target Readership Garden centre decision makers and buyers. Includes owners, directors, managers and other heads of department

Rates Received 1 April 1993 Agency Commission 10%

Standard Rates

mono page £985.00

colour page £1425.00

Mono Rates Mono: Page rop £985.00. Half rop £545.00. Third rop £385.00. Quarter rop £325.00. Series discount 2 10%, 7 15%

Cover Rates by negotiation by negotiation

Colour Rates Full colour: Page rop £1425.00. Half rop £985.00. Third rop £825.00. Quarter rop £765.00. Dps rop £2475.00. 1 standard spot colour: rop £100.00 extra

Inserts Accepted loose by arrangement

Classified Rates Scc rop £16.00. Box no rop £4.50 extra

Production Specifications Type page size 252 × 176, half 252 × 85 or 124 × 176, third 81 × 176, quarter 124 × 85 or 59 × 176. Trim size 297 × 210. Bleed size 307 × 220. Screen: mono 54, colour 60. Sheet fed litho. Mono: film positives, bromide PMT or camera ready artwork. Colour: positive separations, right reading emulsion side down with colour guide

Deadlines Copy 28 days preceding publication date. Cancellation mono 6 weeks, colour 8 weeks preceding publication date

GARDEN AND LEISURE PRODUCTS

Est 1991

Affiliations PPA BBP

Publisher Faversham House Group. Faversham House, 111 St James's Road, Croydon, Surrey, CR2 2TH. Tel 081-684 9659 4082. Fax 081-684 9729

Contacts Editor Marilyn Arthurs, Publishing Director Martin Albert, Sales Director Dan King, Sales Executive (Display) Malcolm Hopwood

Advertisement Sales Tel 081-657 8878

Contacts Sales Executive Stella Garratt

Frequency 3 issues per year Mar Jun Sep

Circulation Uncertified

RES available

Rates Effective 1 January 1992

Standard Rates

colour page £770.00

Colour Rates Full colour: Page rop £770.00. Half rop £400.00. Quarter rop £210.00.

Production Specifications Type page size 190 × 135, half 90 × 135 or 190 × 65, quarter 90 × 65. Trim size 210 × 148. Bleed 213 × 151. Screen: mono 48, colour 54. Film positives, right reading emulsion side down.

Deadlines Copy 15th of month preceding publication date. Cancellation 42 days preceding copy date

Entry amended for this edition

Garden Trade News *International*

THE CHOICE AND VOICE OF THE INDUSTRY

GARDEN TRADE NEWS INTERNATIONAL

Est 1978

Affiliations ABC PPA

Publisher EMAP Apex Publications Ltd. Apex House, Oundle Road, Peterborough, PE2 9NP. Tel 0733 898100. Fax 0733 898418

Contacts Publication Manager David W. Cook, Editor Mike Wyatt

Frequency Monthly 3rd week of month preceding publication date

Editorial Profile Newspaper covering all aspects of garden product retailing. Containing in-depth features on major market sectors plus new product and pet/aquatic sections. Independent of all trade associations

Regular Features *(by BRAD Classification)* Business Management, Horticultural, Marketing, Pet Trade, Retailing

Circulation Jan-Dec 1993 ABC 5,933 (UK 5,913 Overseas 20)

Total net circulation for audit issue 6,259 (UK 6,237 Overseas 22)

	Total	UK	Overseas
Subs total	285	265	20
pd full	280	262	18
pd <100% >50%	5	3	2
Controlled free total	5,961	5,961	0
IR in writing	5,961	5,961	0
Non-controlled free total	13	11	2
by name	13	11	2

Society/Association circulation none

Controlled free circulation terms of control Named individuals and personnel of the following establishments involved in the garden industry: wholesalers, garden centres, nurseries, commercial growers, horticultural merchants, DIY stores, supermarkets, departmental stores, hardware and ironmongery stores, florists and other retailers of garden products.

Age of requests based on the issue distributed on 16/11/93

	1-14mths	15-26mths	27-38mths	total
CC free	1,870	3,138	953	5,961
	31%	53%	16%	100%

Duplication 0% 16/11/93 issue

Variances 0 issues out of 10 varied by more than 10%

Target Readership Owners and managers of garden centres, garden shops, hardware stores, DIY superstores, department stores, supermarkets, garden machinery dealerships and wholesale establishments. Also senior personnel in manufacturing and distribution companies

Rates Effective 1 January 1994 Agency Commission 10%

Standard Rates

mono page £950.00

colour page £1500.00

395 × 296. Screen mono 48, colour 54 reading emulsion side down

Deadlines Copy 5th of month prece[...] to qualified companies

GROUNDCARE MACHINE[...]

Est 1987

Publisher Grassblades Marketing. E[...] horse Street, Baldock, Hertfordshire, S[...] Fax 0462 490066

Contacts Publisher and Editor R. P. Ta[...]

Frequency Monthly

Price Single copy £3

Circulation Uncertified

Rates Effective 1 January 1994 Agenc[...]

Standard Rates

mono page

mono scc

recruitment scc

Mono Rates Mono: Page rop £799.0[...] £729.00 9 £694.00. Half rop £460.[...] £420.00 9 £400.00. Quarter rop £2[...] £221.00 9 £211.00

Cover Rates front page solus by neg[...]

Colour Rates Full colour: rop £350[...] colour: rop £150.00 extra 1 special spo[...]

Bleed Pages 10% extra

Special Positions by negotiation

Inserts By arrangement

Classified Rates Scc rop £10.00. R[...] Box no rop £12.00 extra

Production Specifications Type pag[...] 190, quarter 130 × 93. Trim size 297 × [...] Sheet-fed litho. Mono: bromides or l[...] emusion side down. Colour positives [...] down required, plus proofs and progre[...]

Deadlines Copy 1st of month prece[...]

Advertisement — C[...]

HARDWARE AN[...] GARDEN REVI[...]

Affiliations ABC PPA

LAWN & GARDEN EQUIPM[...]

Est 1988

Publisher Halsbury Publishing, 25A N[...] shire, SP1 2PH. Tel 0722 414245. Fax [...]

Contacts Editor Chris Biddle, Advertis[...]

Frequency Monthly 1st week

Price Single copy £2 Per year £24

Circulation Uncertified

RES available

Rates Effective 1 April 1993 Agency C[...]

Standard Rates

mono page

colour page

Mono Rates Mono: Dps rop £1090.0[...] £925.00, 12 £875.00. Page rop £59[...] £505.00, 12 £480.00. Half rop £3[...] 6 £295.00, 12 £275.00. Quarte[...] £215.00, 6 £200.00, 12 £185.00. E[...] £135.00, 6 £125.00, 12 £115.0[...]

Cover Rates Mono: Quarter page sc[...] Quarter page solus outside back £67[...] solus outside front £700.00. Full [...] £1075.00.

Colour Rates 1 standard spot colo[...] colour: Dps rop £1515.00, series 3 £[...] £1300.00. Page rop £995.00 se[...] £905.00, 12 £880.00. Half rop £720[...] £670.00, 12 £650.00. Quarter [...] £540.00, 6 £525.00, 12 £510.00

Bleed Pages 10% extra

Special Positions facing matter 15%[...]

Inserts Accepted, 2 pages (single sh[...] £825

Classified Rates Lineage semi displ[...] rop £12.00, box no £10.00

Conditions and notes 1 standard spo[...] blue

Production Specifications Type pag[...] 187 or 267 × 89, quarter 130 × 89 or 64 [...] 187. Trim size 297 × 210. Bleed size 31[...] width 44 (4 cols) 59 (3 cols). No of cols [...] Web offset. Colour: emulsion side dow[...] separation planning etc charged extra

Deadlines Copy mono 15 days [...] publication date. Cancellation 4 we[...] date

Entry amended for this edition

NURSERYMAN & GARDEN[...]

Official Business Magazine of t[...] Association

Incorporating Garden Centre, Trad[...] man and Glasshouse Grower

Est 1894

Affiliations ABC PPA BBP

Publisher Bouverie Publishing Co Lt[...] bers, Temple Avenue, London, EC4Y [...] 071-583 4068

Contacts Editor Peter Dawson, Publis[...] vertisement Manager Iona Spencer, Di[...] tine Smart, Classified Sales James Lig[...]

Frequency Fortnightly 2nd and 4th [...]

Price Per year £44

Special Features

2 May 1994	Centenary spe[...]
1 June 1994	Nursery stock s[...] tries review
2 June 1994	Woking catalog[...]
1 July 1994	Pack trials revie[...]

Circulation Jan-Dec 1993 ABC 3,932 [...]

Total net circulation for audit issue 3,77[...]

A page of BRAD directory; as you can see it gives you all the information you could possibly want. Reproduced by kind permission of British Rate and Data.

Researching your customers

This is where you find out all the things you couldn't look up in the library or find in the trade press. The responses to your own specific product or service: the response to the price you were thinking of charging, or the particular method of delivery you wanted to use, or the name you had in mind for the company.

The first thing you need to do is to break your customers down into separate market groups. So for your garden climbing frames you want to research four different groups of customers: private gardeners, garden centres, garden designers and corporate and municipal customers. You may have only one target market for your product or service, but if you have more you must treat them separately. Private gardeners might want much smaller frames than municipal parks do, and garden designers might be much more price sensitive than garden centres – after all, they've got to charge the end customer for assembling and erecting the frames as well.

Rule two of low cost marketing is *talk*. This kind of research is actually relatively inexpensive if you do it yourself – your main costs are your time, and phone or travelling expenses. As long as you follow the basic guidelines, you should get valuable results without having to go to the professionals. Unless you are just setting up in business, there are three categories of people you can research:

- current customers, to find out why they buy from you rather than your competitors
- ex-customers, to find out why they switched to buying from your competitors
- potential customers, to find out what would persuade them to buy from you.

As well as talking to these three groups of people, you can also talk to other people who are in close and frequent contact with them, such as retailers, dealers, agents, trade press and so on. And of course your own telephone sales team or retail staff, who could probably tell you a lot about why your customers buy what they do, if you asked them. Lord Marks used to insist that Marks and Spencer's top people visited one of their stores every week to talk to the counter staff about customer actions and responses.

WHO ARE YOU GOING TO TALK TO?

Ideally, if money were no object, you would talk to everyone who uses your product or service, who has used it in the past or might conceivably use it in the future. Well, the likes of us can forget about that. It's far too expensive. But if we can only afford to telephone 50 people, they'd better be the right 50.

This might not be a problem. If you're a local builder and you need to talk to all the architects in your area, it probably won't cost that much. But if you're manufacturing garden climbing frames and you want to survey every gardener in Britain, it probably will. If you can only afford (or only need) to talk to a selected sample of people, there are essentially two types, known to the professionals as:

- random sample
- quota sample.

The random sample is, for example, a cross-section of all the gardeners in Britain. The quota sample would be architects who work in your area – you'll have other customers as well, so this is targeted research.

It's worth being consciously aware which of these types of research you're doing. Targeted research can usually be kept pretty low cost. But if you are conducting random research on a small scale, you need to work very hard to keep it as random as possible or the results could be very misleading. Suppose you try to keep the cost of your research down by only interviewing local gardeners about your climbing frames. The response may not be representative at all. For instance:

- you may be based in a more affluent area than most
- you might be in a rural area, and city gardeners have different needs

- your area could be very windswept, so the local gardeners have a greater need than most for fencing, which acts as a windbreak.

Perhaps you could take a couple of days out to travel to different parts of the country and interview people as they leave garden centres; or talk to people who visit your stand at a national exhibition. The important thing is to recognise that your research may not be as accurate as you would like. Once you are aware of this you have three options:

1 abandon it before you start and find a completely fresh approach
2 do the research but use its results with caution
3 find some way to make the sample more random (such as travelling elsewhere in the country).

The best way to choose which option to take is to:

- calculate the cost of the research you are thinking of doing
- decide how accurate you need the results to be
- work out the potential earnings/savings that the results of the research could generate.

So if you're using the research to establish whether or not it's worth going ahead with a mailing to all the plumbers in southern England, how much money would that mailing waste if the result of the research is that plumbers are not a viable market? And how much is it likely to make if the answer is yes, plumbers will jump at this product? Balance this against the cost of the research and its level of accuracy and it should be clear whether to go ahead with it or not.

WHAT SORT OF QUESTIONS SHOULD YOU ASK?

Whoever you are talking to, there are two basic approaches: postal surveys or questionnaires, and interviews (which could be face-to-face or on the phone). Large scale surveys or questionnaires involving people with clipboards are expensive, and if you do use them it is almost invariably cheaper to commission them than to do them yourself. But whichever method you use, you will largely be asking people questions. So what questions are you going to ask?

Well, you've already listed the questions you want answered, so all you really need to do is rephrase them so that the people you are asking can answer them easily. There are certain general rules you need to follow to make sure you get the results you want.

Don't assume certain questions are unnecessary

It may be that your guess will be pretty accurate, but don't assume it, *think* about it. When the training film company Video Arts first started, they decided to make a pair of films for retailers to train their shop assistants in handling customers face-to-face. They knew there was a market – they'd been into enough shops where the assistants clearly didn't have a clue how to deal with customers to realise that. However, what they didn't know was that no-one in the retail industry spent any money on training shop assistants in the early 1970s. Fortunately, they found this out just in time and changed the settings in the film to places like travel agents, banks, airport check-ins and hotels – areas of the market where companies were training people in customer care.

Are you sure customers want what you think they want?

Joe Hyman, the legendary textile entrepreneur, took over Gainsborough Cornard, an East Anglian textile mill, in the 1960s. While reconstructing the factory he took a lot of orders based on a wide choice of colourways. And then, just as the factory was about to come on stream, the Council stepped in. The whole plan hinged on having two dyeing vats: no, they said, the drainage system won't take it. They could only have one vat.

Disaster! The range of colourways depended on two vats. Now the range had to be halved. In desperation they told their customers. There was a certain amount of disappointment, but every customer who had ordered one of the cancelled colours just changed to one of the others. Not a single order was lost, and running only one vat dramatically reduced the company's production costs.

You may think your customers want a choice of 12 colours, or an option on emergency delivery, but check. If they don't, you could save yourself a fortune.

Avoid making implicit assumptions

Suppose you ask people 'Would you prefer to have goods assembled for you on site or would you prefer to assemble them yourself?' It sounds like a fair question, and if they have a preference they will doubtless state it. But in fact, they might have preferred to have the goods arrive ready assembled. Then they don't have to do it themselves or hang around while someone does it for them. So make sure you offer *all* the options.

Don't ask leading questions

Rather than 'Would you prefer eight-foot climbing frames to six-foot ones?' ask 'Which would you prefer: eight-foot or six-foot frames?'

Use clear, comprehensible questions

Make sure the people you are questioning can understand all the questions easily. As well as using plain language, this may also mean grouping them into logical sections. Explain the question if you think it will help, either orally in interviews or on paper if they are completing a questionnaire themselves.

Don't be vague or ambiguous

For example, don't say 'Do you spend a lot of time in the garden?' Their idea of a lot may not be yours. Better to ask 'How many hours a week do you spend in the garden?' It is a good idea to divide this into sections (for example: less than one hour a week, one to three hours, and so on) with boxes to tick if they're filling out the questionnaire themselves. Otherwise it will take you far longer to sort out the responses, when everyone gives you a slightly different answer.

So there are the main points that are worth remembering when you're compiling questions for either surveys or interviews. Here's a quick summary checklist.

Compiling questions for surveys and interviews

1 Don't assume certain questions are unnecessary.
2 Are you sure customers want what you think they want?
3 Avoid making implicit assumptions.
4 Don't ask leading questions.
5 Use clear, comprehensible questions.
6 Don't be vague or ambiguous.

POSTAL QUESTIONNAIRES

You must have been sent self-completion questionnaires in the past. Do you fill them in? How do you decide which ones to complete? Is there anything that really irritates you about any of them? One of the most useful things you can do is to follow your own experience of filling in questionnaires.

Encouraging people to complete the questionnaire

One of the most important points is to make sure people actually complete and return them at all. I suspect you'll find that you are more likely to fill in a questionnaire or survey form if you know and like the company that sent it. You can expect a higher response rate from loyal, long-standing customers than from people who have never heard of you. If you're sending questionnaires to people who don't know you or your company, don't be surprised if you get a response rate in the region of 1–2%. But apart from the sample of people you survey, how can you maximise the response rate?

- Write a brief introduction to attract people's interest.
- You could offer an incentive for filling out the form – a 5% discount on the next purchase, or a free gift (if you're thinking of doing this, make sure that the value of the information is greater than the value of the incentive). Or put returned forms

into a draw and give the winner a magnum of champagne – it's cheaper than a free gift for everyone.

■ You could try faxing the questionnaire in order to grab attention.

■ The shorter it is the better. Try to stick to one sheet of paper at the most, about six to eight questions, and a maximum of about five minutes' completion time.

■ Make the layout simple and clear, with lots of space, and print it on a paper of reasonable quality.

■ Only ask questions that are relevant. This may seem obvious, but a surprising number of companies put in extra, irrelevant questions simply because they think they're interesting, or because they want to mislead any competitors who chance upon the questionnaire.

■ If possible, tell them you'll let them know the results if they contribute (this particularly applies to customers) – and remember to do it.

35

Closed questions

There are two basic types of questions you can ask: closed and open. Closed questions give people the following options in answering:

■ yes or no
■ multiple choice (tick box)
■ scales – giving your response to a statement on a scale of 1 (strongly agree) to 5 (strongly disagree).

These kinds of questions are useful if you are questioning a lot of people, and they make it far easier to computerise and interpret the results as each question has a fixed number of possible answers.

Open questions

Open questions, such as 'What do you look for in a supplier?', can have almost as many answers as there are returned questionnaires. The main advantage of these questions is that they contain no bias, and you often get longer and more in-depth replies. The chief disadvantage is that the answers are more complicated to analyse, so they're better when you're asking only a small number of people.

Piloting the questionnaire

The only way to be sure that your questionnaire is clear and simple to fill in, and can generate answers that are useful to you, is to test it. Give it to about half a dozen people to fill in. These could be people on your target list, or they could be friends or colleagues. If they are colleagues, though, make sure they know nothing about the subject of this questionnaire. Otherwise they might understand questions that your target respondents won't.

INTERVIEWS

We said earlier that large scale questionnaires (asked by people with clipboards) are best handled by the professionals, if you need to do them. At the same time, it's a good idea to do some small scale research of this type yourself, even if only for the occasional odd hour or two. It can give you some surprising insights, as well as helping you understand the limitations of this kind of research. If you're compiling your own questionnaire, you can refine it a lot if you try your questions out in the high street or on the doorstep. This type of interview is essentially a questionnaire, so you can follow the same basic guidelines as for postal questionnaires.

The other type of interview is the more in-depth variety. This is useful if you want to contact up to about 40 people – it starts to get a little too time-consuming after that (unless there are several of you conducting the interviews). For this you can either make appointments to see people, or telephone them. You usually find that you can tell how many of these interviews to carry out, because after a while you can feel that you have stopped learning anything new.

This type of interview is invaluable for the feeling you get from speaking to people yourself. You will pick up nuances of tone that you cannot get from a postal questionnaire or agency research reports. 'It's a good system' could be said to imply it's workable, although others are better, or it could imply that it's excellent. It's hard to exaggerate the value of this kind of research, even if you do combine it with other types. And you have an advantage over rich organisations that can afford to use agencies all the time as they are missing out on an invaluable chance to gain an intuitive feel for their customers.

It also means that if someone makes a point slightly out of the range of your planned questions, but clearly useful anyway, you can take a couple of minutes out to explore it. They may have some useful ideas that are worth further research.

Probably the most useful approach to this kind of interview, if you are doing it yourself, is a semi-structured approach. You ask certain questions of everyone, including some closed questions (these results will be easier to collate). But you also leave room for some unstructured discussion of any points or ideas that seem worth exploring. There are a couple of general tips worth noting for conducting interviews:

37

- if you're on the phone, try to plan an interview that will take between five and ten minutes (maybe fifteen at the most). When you ring, let the interviewee know how long it will take, ask if they're busy at the moment and, if they are, arrange an appointment to telephone again at a time when they'll be free

- you often find that it takes a while to write down the answers to open questions. However, it can seem rude, especially on the phone, to leave the interviewee twiddling their thumbs while you finish writing another two paragraphs, so try this tip: have a list of open questions that sound relevant, but to which you don't need to know the answer. When you get behind with recording the interviewee's last answer, ask them a question from this list. Then, under the guise of writing down the answer, you can actually finish writing the answer to the previous question

- whatever you do, don't attempt to combine interviewing and selling. If the interviewee is really interested in your product or service, they'll ask for more information. But they are doing you a favour by giving up their time to speak to you, so don't be tempted to abuse this by trying to sell to them – think how you'd feel in their position.

Recording the interviews

In order to be able to interpret the results of your research, you will need to keep good records. Write up an index card or a record sheet for each interview as soon as possible after it. It is hard to believe just how fast you can simply forget the information, or confuse interviews in your mind, if you don't do this. You will need to record:

- the details of the interviewee: company (if relevant), name, address, job title
- the date
- the answers given to each question
- additional notes on the interview.

ANALYSING THE RESULTS

It's hard to give clear guidelines here because it depends very much on the questions. You will discover at this point, if you haven't already, if any of your questions were unclear. If you've asked an ambiguous question to which one person has answered '3' and another has replied 'the production manager' you will have a hard time collating the responses.

But assuming the questions were well designed, you need to ask yourself two questions:

1 'What do I want to know?' and, for each thing you want to know,
2 'In what format do I want the answer?'

Obviously you will want to know the answers to the questions on the list (or why were they there?), but you may want to know other things as well. For example, of the people who say they would like more climbing plants in their gardens, how many also said they like climbers to look tidy? Make sure you get all the useful information you can, including cross-referencing questions.

It's usually quite easy to work out what form you want the answer in; the important thing is to ask yourself. Otherwise you'll generate all your results as lists or tables. Just consider, for each question, which of these formats would be the most helpful:

- list
- average (range, mean, median or mode)
- table
- chart (such as a bar chart)
- pie chart
- graph.

TEST MARKETING

Ultimately, the best instrument of research is a product. People might tell you all sorts of things about what they might spend if . . . , but in the end they vote with their chequebooks.

If you are starting a new business or launching a new product or service, it is often a good idea to start off locally (assuming you're not manufacturing, say, battleships). This is a form of test marketing that keeps down your costs (delivery, advertising and so on) until you have ironed out the creases and are ready to expand.

Not surprisingly, test marketing bears a lot of similarity to choosing samples for questionnaires. You need to be aware that your locality (or wherever you choose to test the product) may not be representative of the total market; try to choose somewhere that is as representative as possible if you go out of your own area, but either way don't expect the results to be borne out exactly when you go national or international.

Remember also that the bigger the test area, the more accurate the results – and the more expensive the exercise. So apply the usual rule: how accurate do we *need* to be? And don't pay for a bigger test than you have to in order to achieve that level of accuracy.

Researching your competitors

You've got to know what you're up against. How do you know someone else isn't already producing stronger plant climbing frames cheaper than you can make yours? Or ones that are easier to assemble? You need to monitor the competition continuously; they could bring out a new product tomorrow, or next Monday – if you're not watching them you won't be ready to react.

You also need to be aware of exactly what you are competing with – you may have more competition than you think. Look at this list of what our plant climbing frames and fencing might be competing against:

- other metal climbing frames
- other fencing for training plants on, such as trellises
- traditional fencing (without plants trained on it)
- frames that people improvise at no cost – tree stumps, interesting shaped pieces of ironwork reclaimed from skips and so on
- topiary bushes to give shape and height to the garden.

Your other main competitor in just about any market is the option of having nothing at all. There will be some gardeners who just don't like climbing plants. So not only do you want to win new business by persuading gardeners that your product is better than your competitors', you also want to persuade other gardeners to revise their attitude to climbing plants.

Once you've identified your competitors, how do you find out what they're up to and what their customers think of them? There are lots of ways to get hold of the information you want. Some of them may seem unfair at first, but you're only using freely available information, and if they're doing their job properly, they'll be doing the same thing to you. Try:

- the library again – look them up in the trade directories to find out who they are and what they do
- the competitors themselves – ring them and ask for information/brochures/quotes and so on, send off coupons in reply to their advertisements, visit their stands at exhibitions, collect point-of-sale material from their retail outlets, get hold of a copy of their annual report. Notice the service they provide – does the literature arrive promptly? How friendly are their staff over the phone?
- trade press – read the general or trade press and look at their advertisements or any editorial on them
- their customers – when you conduct a survey, ask customers what they would like their suppliers to add to their current service, or what they particularly value about their present supplier
- their suppliers – talk to the people who supply them; they may know a lot about them, like their reputation, how fast they pay and so on.

It's a good idea to research your competitors after you've researched the market (though you may want to survey customers only once, and combine questions about your competitors with other questions). Judge them against the factors that your research has identified as being important to customers – price, speed of delivery, product range or whatever. This helps to prevent bias, which can be a big problem; there's a great temptation to view the competition critically because we *want* them to be doing a poor job. This is a dangerous approach. Conversely, it will do no harm at all to overestimate them. It's well worth making a list of each competitor's good and bad points, because then you have to look for the good ones consciously.

Listening to the answers

One of the commonest mistakes people make is to ignore or misinterpret the results of their research because they don't want to hear it. It's quite understandable. You've got really excited about your new business, product, service or whatever – and the research suggests that your potential customers aren't anywhere near as excited about it as you. It's very tempting to gloss over that bit of the research or make excuses for it: 'Well, we didn't phrase the questions that well', 'But, of course, that research was local; you'd expect the market in the South East to be much better.'

It's far better to take a different, more positive attitude: you've been successful in getting a clear answer to your questions. Why else were you asking them? And a result that appears negative may not be that bad anyway. The research may be indicating that your original idea is not as promising as you'd thought, but it could be that a rethink about price, packaging, sales outlets or something else could resolve the problem. If that's the case, the research has saved you a fortune that you might have wasted on trying to sell a product that wasn't quite right for the market.

The Wildlife Trusts are a group of around 50 independent wildlife trusts around the country. These trusts each recruit members locally in their own county. The Wildlife Trusts thought it would be far more efficient to recruit members centrally, through a single national membership drive. They could advertise in wildlife magazines, mail people direct and so on. They were quite right – it would cost far less than lots of separate, local membership campaigns.

But before they went ahead with it, they had the sense to carry out some research. In true low cost marketing style, they centred this on existing information and past research on similar subjects in order to keep new research to a minimum. The results showed them something no-one had expected. Almost all wildlife trust members were recruited face-to-face, at exhibitions and events or on the doorstep. A centralised advertising and mailshot campaign would be a very expensive way to achieve very little.

Far from being a failed membership campaign, this was in fact a highly successful piece of research that gave The Wildlife Trusts exactly what they wanted – a clear answer to the question 'Could we recruit more members at less cost if we co-ordinated the campaign centrally?'

Most research will produce some answers that you didn't expect. So once you've completed it, you'll need to go back and revise the marketing plan you drew up in Chapter 1. And since market research should be a continual exercise, that means that you will need at least to review your marketing plan, and possibly to revise it, regularly throughout its life.

THE FINAL RESULT

43

So what could market research have told us about the climbing frames for plants? We've done the desk research, we've interviewed potential customers, sent questionnaires to garden centres, and talked to landscape gardeners on the phone. We've also interviewed council officers and company buyers face-to-face. And we checked out the other products on the market.

Desk research

- *The library* We looked up lists of landscape gardening companies, garden centres, big local companies (to keep costs down we'll need to start locally, a form of test marketing).
- *The trade press* We found out the details of all the specialist gardening magazines and the gardening trade publications, and got them to send us a media pack, including a copy of their latest issue.

Researching our customers

- *Interviewing potential customers* We talked to nearly 200 people in garden centre car parks, and asked them all half a dozen preset questions.

- *Surveying garden centres* We sent out a printed questionnaire to 100 garden centres in the region. We wrote a chatty, friendly introduction that explained briefly that we were a new company with a new product. We only asked six questions (and left space in case they wanted to add comments), and said we'd let them know the results. Of the 100, 30 replied.

- *Interviewing landscape gardeners* We spent about 10 minutes on the phone to each of 20 landscape gardeners. We asked about ten set questions, and then encouraged them to talk in-depth for a few minutes.

- *Interviewing council officers and commercial buyers* We spoke to about five council officers and eight company buyers face-to-face, for about 15 minutes each. Again, we asked about ten set questions, then talked in a less structured way for the rest of the interview.

Researching our competitors

- *Reading the trade press* We found out who our competitors were and how they advertised to gardeners, their prices, the benefits they promoted and so on.

- *Contacting the competitors* We asked them to send us brochures, and we looked at their products in garden centres and at exhibitions.

- *Talking to garden centres* We found out what was their most popular competitive product at present, and why.

- *Talking to customers* We asked them what their priorities were, and which products fulfilled them. We found out how many of them grew climbing plants, what they trained them on, and what kind of fencing or screening they preferred.

Listening to the answers

At the end of it all, we came up with some interesting answers:

- we could not produce our frames and fences cheaply enough to compete at the bottom end of the market

- a considerable part of the market was not very price sensitive; these people would rather pay more for a product they thought was of a better quality and looked classier.

These factors taken together suggest that we should produce high quality frames and fences for the top end of the market.

We then tried out two names: *Frame-up* and *Arabesque*. The response showed that potential customers saw *Frame-up* as a relatively hi-tech, cheap and cheerful product. They saw *Arabesque* as more expensive and stylish.

In view of the discovery that we should aim at the top end of the market, let's call ourselves Arabesque (after checking at Companies House that we can legally do so, of course).

We also discovered that people were quite happy with a choice of only three designs of free-standing frames, and one of fencing/ screening. They wanted fencing about four feet high, although parks and commercial companies wanted six-foot high fencing.

It seems that this relatively small range of designs is enough, and it's certainly cheaper to produce. The response from commercial companies was encouraging, too, so it seems wise to be able to offer them six-foot high screening.

We found that one of the most frequent complaints about currently available frames and fences is that they are heavy and cumbersome.

Since our frames will be made of hollow aluminium and are easy to erect, this will be a strong selling point.

The unstructured part of the telephone and face-to-face interviews turned up a couple of useful pieces of information we'd never have learned otherwise:

- parks and businesses liked the idea of matching archways to put into a run of fencing in order to create a way through. This should not be too expensive to produce in a single design
- people preferred the idea of coated metal to bare metal, for colour (dull green was preferred) and because they felt it would wear better. They also pointed out that plants would need a

45

rough surface to hold on to. This point suggests that we should research methods, and costs, of coating the aluminium tubing with a textured material.

So that's research – except, of course, that's never really it. Market research continues as long as the business continues, because its function has as much to do with running an established business as it does with starting a new one.

3

Pricing

If one has not made a reasonable profit, one has made a mistake.

Li Xiannian

There are many people who take the view that pricing has nothing to do with marketing. It is true that there are aspects of pricing – complex calculations, forecasts, risk calculations – that seem to have little to do with it, but the final price you arrive at is central to the marketing. It sets the standard by which your customers (and potential customers) will judge you.

If you paid £250 for a new pair of shoes and the soles wore through after a fortnight, you'd probably be livid and go straight back to the shop demanding a refund. But if you'd paid only £2.50 for them you'd probably just shrug and think, 'Well, you get what you pay for.' Quite right too. You assume that a £250 pair of shoes will be of irreproachable quality, while a pair that cost only £2.50 were never likely to last very long.

In the same way, if your products or services are priced higher than the competition, your customers will assume that they are better. If they are cheaper, your customers will expect quality (or lack of it) to match. In fact, the price you set is one of the strongest marketing signals you can give.

Price and the market

The higher your price, the louder you're telling your customers that your product or service is high quality. But of course, that might not be a good thing.

ARE YOUR CUSTOMERS MORE SENSITIVE TO PRICE OR TO QUALITY?

If your customers are more sensitive to price than quality, they would rather buy from your cheaper competitors. Suppose you're selling brown envelopes – the best envelopes, and the most expensive to prove it. You might find that most of your customers can't really tell the difference between one brown envelope and the next. They just want something to put their letters in before they post them. They walk into the shop, pick up the cheapest packet they can find, and hey presto! – you're out of business.

On the other hand, you could be selling elegant, expensive sofas. Anyone contemplating buying from you or your competitors is expecting to pay a lot of money. They are probably far more concerned about the quality of the furniture than the price. So if your higher price suggests a better quality, they may well buy from you.

CAN YOU LIVE UP TO YOUR CUSTOMERS' EXPECTATIONS?

If you price your goods or services high enough to imply that your quality is exceptional, you're going to have a fairly irate bunch of customers on your hands if you can't live up to their expectations. Remember the example of the shoes? If people pay extra, it's because they expect to get more. You've got to give it to them, at a cost that you can afford.

The extra you give them doesn't have to be the quality of the goods specifically. It could be the speed of delivery, the standard of service, the payment terms – but it's got to be something the customer recognises as being worth the extra money.

THE PSYCHOLOGY OF PRICING

You can't assume that people will choose one product over another on purely rational grounds. Some people will choose a more expensive product because they like the packaging better, or because it's what their mother always used to buy. When you look at products like washing powders and detergents, you often find that one manufacturer is selling the same product under two different brand names at two different prices. There's no hard, logical reason for buying the more expensive brand, but enough people *think* it's better in some way for it to sell.

The psychology of your own market

Some markets allow for a greater range of prices than others. In some markets you'll find that the cheapest product costs only a few per cent less than the dearest – laser printers, for example, or ¾″ screws. In other cases, the difference is enormous: people expect a new outfit to cost anywhere between about £5 and £5000. If you're in toothpaste, your viable price range just isn't going to be as great as it is in, say, the hotel business.

49

Price plateaux

People tend to see prices in bands. A certain item costs 'between £10 and £15'. The larger the amount of money, the wider the band. So people might regard anything between 10p and 19p as being in the same band, but if they're buying a house they might regard £135 000 and £149 000 as being in the same bracket – even though there is actually £14 000 difference between them.

To a large extent, people will buy a product they want so long as it's in the right price band. In other words, they'll pay £19.95 for just about anything they would have paid £18.95 for – they simply regard them both as being 'a bit under £20' (certain sums, such as £20, are known as 'price barriers'). This, of course, is why so many products are priced at £2.99, £49.90, £99.50 and so on – to keep them in the lower price bracket. So if you reckon you can sell your product profitably at £46, the chances are you can sell just as many at £49.90. Don't take my word for it, but do check it out.

Fixing the price

If you're going to stay in business, you've got to charge more for your goods than it costs to make them – that's pretty obvious. So the first thing you need to know is what your costs are – the basic question and, in every sense, the bottom line. There are more costs to take into account than many people allow for, so here's a run down of the main considerations to bear in mind.

WHAT IS EACH ONE GOING TO COST TO MAKE?

Not as straightforward as it sounds, because making a thousand does not cost ten times as much as making a hundred – there are economies of volume. But you can work out the different unit costs for different production volumes; the higher the volume the lower the unit cost.

WHAT WILL IT COST US TO SELL?

Whereas most people are pretty good at calculating production costs, most people wildly underestimate selling costs. They can include:

- creating and printing sales literature and catalogues
- mailing
- telephoning
- sales journeys and sales calls
- staff costs
- discounts
- correspondence
- exhibitions and point-of-sale displays
- advertising
- public relations
- one of the most frequently overlooked selling costs is 'dry holes' – proposals, estimates, quotations and conversations that don't eventually lead to any business.

WHAT WILL IT COST TO DISTRIBUTE?

Just postage and packaging? Will you need a commercial carrier?

Do you need to buy or hire a delivery van?

WILL WE SELL THROUGH INTERMEDIARIES?

If you're going to sell through agents, retailers or other inter-mediaries whom you don't control, you must take into account the profit margin they will need to make it worth buying, and still cheap enough to sell on.

WHAT WILL OUR OVERHEADS BE?

If you are starting a business from scratch, you may be able to do a lot yourself and from home. But if you are already part of an established business you won't have these cost savings. In any case, if your new business goes well you may have to take on staff and premises later. That means rent, Council Tax, insurance, salaries, heat, light, telephone, office equipment, postage, stationery and repairs. Either way there'll be bookkeeper's costs, bank charges, and the cost of someone's time filling out tax returns, VAT and other government regulations, and forms for compliance and completion.

51

It is a catch because if you have based your prices on the cost of working from home or from your current site, expansion may hit your profit margins. So you have to think about overheads even if you are not incurring them at all initially. And even if you're starting up on your own, working from home, you must include the cost of your own time in your calculations. Otherwise what will you live on? Even if you don't need an income to start with, you don't want to have to put your prices up later simply in order to pay yourself.

WILL THERE BE PROFESSIONAL COSTS?

Will you need an accountant or tax adviser? Will you need a solicitor to set up a limited company? What about patents, trade-marks, copyright and licences? Do you need any form of public liability insurance? The answer may be no, but you still have to ask the question.

HOW LONG WILL WE HAVE TO WAIT FOR OUR MONEY?

Best of all is cash with order; you actually get the money before you send the goods – perhaps even before you acquire them, or the raw materials to make them. Worst is sale or return; you may have to take all the stock back. Services are usually better than manufactured goods, because you usually don't have too many suppliers to pay while you're waiting for your customers to pay you. Selling for cash over the counter is good, especially if you can get credit from your suppliers. But payment in 30, 60 or 90 days can be a real pain, especially if you find yourself devoting more time to chasing late payers than expanding the business. And it all puts up your costs, which may lead to a price increase as well to cover it.

Don't forget, either, the cost of chasing debtors: invoices, statements, reminders, phone calls, lawyers' letters.

HOW WILL WE COPE WITH SUCCESS?

We've already looked at the technical problems of expanding production, but it has a cash dimension too. Perhaps you can finance expansion from retained earnings, which is the soundest way. But perhaps you can't. You may have to borrow, and interest charges then become a factor in production costs. Or you may want to bring in a partner with cash. Perhaps the need won't occur for years, but thinking about it may suggest putting out feelers quite early on.

WHAT IS OUR BREAK-EVEN POINT?

This is the crunch question, and it hasn't got an answer. Or, rather, it has several answers. 500 units priced at £50 each, will bring you a gross of £25 000 a year. Will that cover all the costs of producing 500 a year? What about 2000 units at £40 each? Could you do that for £80 000?

At the beginning it's all guesswork, but you absolutely have to know how many units you have to sell at whatever price you decide on if you are to keep a proper distance between yourself and the Official Receiver. And of course the number you need to sell will have a profound effect on your marketing plan.

Perhaps the easiest approach is to draw a simple graph. Work out the total cost for producing one unit a week (that's *all* the fixed costs, plus the variable costs for one item). So if it costs you £500 to sit in your office for a week and twiddle your thumbs, and the extra cost for making one unit is £5, the total cost of the first unit will be £505. The total cost of making two units will be £510.

Along the bottom of your graph, mark off the volume (in ones, tens, hundreds or whatever is most appropriate for your business). Up the side of the graph mark the total costs. Then, calculate the total cost for each volume marked along the bottom, and mark that point on the graph (see example below). Don't assume that it will climb smoothly, because your variable costs could change according to volume. It may be that if you are ordering enough raw materials to produce 400 items a week, you

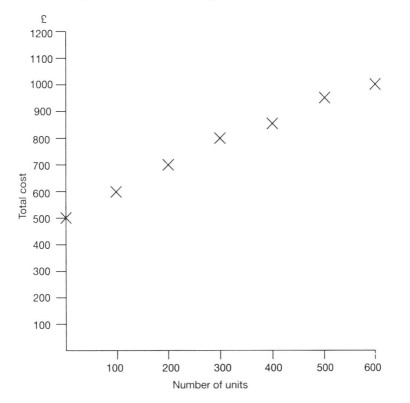

will get a bulk discount from your suppliers, which will reduce your costs. But other costs will increase, and increase suddenly – you can't keep adding 10% of a secretary or an office until you've got a whole one. Variable costs climb a slope, but fixed costs climb a staircase.

Join the marks on your graph to form a line (see example below). Any price *above* that line represents profit; any price *below* it signifies commercial suicide. Suppose you think you can sell 200 units a week. Follow the 200-unit mark upwards, and where it crosses the line is the amount of money you must bring in to break even. Just divide the amount by 200 to give you the unit price.

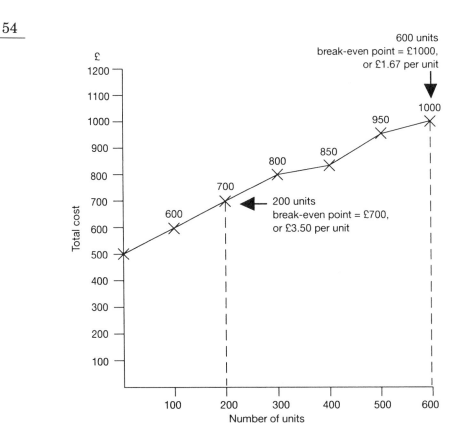

Your research should give you a strong indication of what price the market will bear. But don't forget that the price can determine the market. If you double the price of your goods, you could start to appeal far more to the top end of the market. So you can sell fewer units and still make more profit – or, as often happens, sell even more units.

Here's a perfect example of the way that choosing a different point along the cost/volume scale can shift you into a different market completely.Tom Maschler, Managing Director of Jonathan Cape, brought off the publishing coup of the seventies with a book called *And Miss Carter Wore Pink*. Miss Carter's paintings were charming, primitive representations of life in the North of England at the turn of the century, with her own brief commentary on each picture, and Tom Maschler felt they would appeal to a much larger public than the normal art book readership – especially if he included text, to make it more than just an art book.

55

So instead of printing about 4000 copies, he took his courage in both hands and printed 40 000. This meant he could sell it at a quarter of the normal price for a book with two dozen full-colour plates. It sold out.

DON'T SELL YOURSELF SHORT

When you fix your price, remember that it is always easier to lower prices than to raise them. If you discover later that you could have sold just as many units at 50% more, it's going to be hard to change when you've built up a customer base that expects your lower price. If you start off pricing too high, however, they're hardly likely to complain when you drop your prices.

It's surprising how often businesses launch new products at a lower price than they need to. It's probably the biggest single mistake people make in pricing. In fact, a higher price often increases your sales, because it positions you in a different, and less price sensitive, market.

After Eight mints are a good illustration of this. They discovered that there was a market gap for an upmarket, sophisticated after-dinner chocolate. The market for kids, office workers' coffee breaks, gift boxes and so on was almost saturated – but there was nothing with the image of silver glinting in the candlelight and reflected from the polished mahogany. After Eights were able to enter the market at a relatively high price because of the market they were aiming for. In fact, if they had priced themselves much lower, they would have had less credibility in that market.

To give you another example, J. Lyons & Co. sold five grades of tea before the First World War, priced at 2d, 4d, 6d, 8d and 10d. The two most expensive teas were absolutely identical – the directors all drank the 8d version – but they sold a lot of the 10d packs none the less.

When should you raise your price?

Every market is different. There are no hard and fast rules. But as a guideline, you should consider putting a higher price on your product or service if any of these conditions apply:

- it is unique
- it is heavily advertised
- customers will only get value from it if they invest a lot of time in learning how to use it
- the market is too small to attract competitors
- you have evidence that customers are willing to pay a higher price.

Of course the higher your prices, the fewer units you have to shift to make a profit. Low cost marketing is far easier if you are in a low-volume, high-margin business than if you are producing a large volume of goods at a low margin. This is because high-volume production brings with it all sorts of production management, finance management and personnel management headaches.

Changing the price

Why would you need to change your prices once you've fixed them (apart from raising them in line with inflation)? Well, there are several reasons why you might *want* to change your prices, all of them probably aimed at increasing turnover. But there are two basic reasons why you would *have* to think about a price change. If you want to retain a constant profit margin, you will have to change the price if your income drops, or if your costs rise.

INCOME IS DROPPING

This could happen for lots of reasons, all to do with the state of the market – the product is becoming obsolete, there are new competitors, the market is flooded or a hundred other causes. You need to find out the reason before you do anything else. If the reason is that your customers have discovered that your product doesn't work, the answer is to fix the product, not change the price. But a price change can often solve the problem. Remember, though, that if you drop your price it will be very hard to raise it again later. However, if a lower price would increase your volume of sales, it could be the answer to this problem.

Contrary to what you might think, raising your price could also increase your sales. This is because you are effectively 'repositioning' yourself in the market. You are sending a different message to your customers and cultivating a different image. You might even be entering a new market, for example moving from selling blackboard chalk to selling the same chalk for billiard cues.

COSTS ARE RISING

The reasons here are different. Suppose orders have been increasing steadily and have now reached a level where you can only meet the demand if you move to larger premises or invest in new, expensive equipment. Or you want to take on another three sales people. Or interest rates have gone up.

57

In theory, you have the same options as you do if sales are dropping. However, you have an added complication because the market may be holding steady and, therefore, not in the best state for a price change which will seem inexplicable to your customers. (Unless you can change your price without your customers noticing – we'll look at ways of doing that in a moment.) However, the fact is that your price should be determined by the market. As we all know, this can shift constantly, and may take your price with it (which is why research is a constant and not an occasional activity). But while the market is stable, you should already be charging the best price – and if you're not, why not?

Essentially there are three options here:

1 find savings elsewhere, or accept a cut in your profit margin, and leave the price alone
2 if you have to change the price, change the product to justify it. This could mean making it more cheaply if you want to drop the price and increase the volume, or it could mean adding value to it, changing the packaging, improving the maintenance and after-sales service or whatever, but, whatever it is, doing something that explains the price change to the market
3 avoid the increased costs altogether by raising your prices. In this case you can get away with changing the price in a stable market because you *expect* to lose sales as a result. This is the only valid reason for changing the price without changing the product. But in this case you have calculated that it is more profitable to lose a few sales than to increase your costs.

As an example of this last point, one kennel owner found that he was taking more and more bookings to look after people's dogs while they went on holiday. In the end he started to turn people away because he had no more room. It looked as though he was going to have to build another block of kennels, take on more staff to feed, clean and walk the dogs, increase his administration costs and so on. He did the costings and found that he'd end up with a smaller profit at the end of it all.

So he decided to put his prices up instead. He did some research to check which customers would stay and which would take their dogs somewhere else. He found that all his best, most regular and long standing customers would rather pay the higher price than go somewhere new. So he forgot about the new building work, the extra staff and so on, and put his prices up. Enough customers stayed to keep him constantly busy, but not enough to have to turn any of them away. And, of course, his profits increased dramatically.

HOW TO CHANGE THE PRICE

You don't have to cover up a price sticker that says 50p with one that says 55p. There are plenty of other ways of going about it. Not every technique can be applied to every product or service, but here's an indication of the kinds of approaches you can adopt.

Raising the price without the customers noticing

- Start charging for extras; for example, stop including the batteries in the price, charge extra for delivery, add on expenses to a consultancy bill.
- Introduce higher charges at certain times only; for example, increase ticket prices on Saturday nights.
- Raise the price, but spread it out in instalments; for example, introduce hire-purchase on your washing machines. (When you calculate the increased price, don't forget to allow for the effect on your cash flow, loss of interest on savings, and so on. The fewer instalments, and the closer together, the better. Two instalments a month apart is far better for your cash flow than 24 instalments spread over 2 years.)
- Raise the price, but include 'unlimited use' in it; for example, for facilities in a fitness club, meat in a carvery.

Dropping the price without lowering the customers' image of you

- Include extras at reduced or no cost; for example, batteries included, free delivery.

- Introduce lower charges at specific times only; for example, off-peak phone charges.
- Give discounts on bulk purchases; for example, season tickets.
- Give discounts on top-of-the-range products only; for example, exotic holidays but not European or UK holidays.

Making your prices appear lower without dropping them

- Promote bargains, discounts and so on so that no-one ever pays the full list price; for example, car prices, railway fares or airline tickets.
- Introduce a lower 'trial price'; for example, an introductory subscription rate for a magazine.

TO SUMMARISE

There are really five key rules to pricing:

1 pricing and marketing are inextricably linked
2 always make sure your pricing is market led
3 you must know your break-even point at every volume level, and cost in everything when you calculate it
4 it is harder to raise prices than to lower them
5 don't sell yourself short.

The printed word

Less is more

One of the biggest costs you face in marketing your product or service is the printer's bill. From letterheads to leaflets, brochures to business cards, printing is full of opportunities to save money – or to chuck it away. This chapter will examine how to do the former.

The greatest scope for saving money lies, as usual, in doing as much as you can for yourself. Setting up your own print shop may not be the best idea, but you can write your own material and design it yourself – or at least do some of the design work. If you have a desktop publishing package on your computer you may even be able to prepare the artwork yourself. Once you are ready to print, there are plenty of ways in which to economise at the printer's without cutting back on quality.

In this chapter we will look at the general rules of writing, designing and buying print. These principles apply to all the materials you might want to print, such as:

- stationery
- business cards
- sales brochures
- leaflets
- customer newsletters
- annual reports
- catalogues

- exhibition display boards
- presentation handouts
- signs
- maintenance and instruction manuals
- invoices, delivery notes and so on
- packaging.

Choosing a logo

If you're launching a new company, a new product or brand – or perhaps opening a new division or updating your image – the first thing you want is a logo. If you had money to throw away, you'd go to a highly experienced – and expensive – designer. They'd know all the right questions to ask in order to come up with a clear brief. Then they'd draw up half a dozen alternatives and ask you to pick one (and pay for the other five as well). If you used the right designer it would be worth every penny (if you had any pennies).

If you have a very small budget, but you can afford to hand over one job to a professional designer, ask them to design the logo. You can't manage without a logo, and a good one should soon become instantly recognisable to your existing and potential customers. It sums up the company or the product. Once you've found a successful logo, you will stick with it for years.

However, you may have to design your own logo, in which case don't panic. It doesn't have to be that complicated. Designs can take several different forms and the simple ones can be just as effective as the complex ones. You could use:

- the name or initials of your business or product
- an abstract symbol (like Mercedes cars)
- a simple picture design (such as Penguin books)
- a combination of name and design.

Look at other people's logos. Collect ones you like, and ones you don't. Think about why you feel the way you do about them. Try to work out what they say about their companies.

Some logos say 'we're cheap and cheerful' or 'you can rely on us' or 'our products are high quality'. Try to decide what it is about the logo that gives this message. The colour? The lettering? Use these clues to help you choose your own logo.

You need to ask yourself what message you want to give your

customers about your company or product, and pick a logo that sends this signal (the next chapter looks at your company image in more detail). The important thing here is to pick only one message – or, if you really must, two at the very most – to send out. You might want to say that your product or service is a high-quality one. Or hi-tech, imaginative, comfortable, fast, cheap, stylish, reliable . . . whatever you think will attract customers the most. You might *want* to say all these things, but unfortunately it won't work – people will just get confused. It's worth spending time choosing your message; follow the proven low cost techniques of thinking about it and talking it over with people whose judgement you value.

COLOUR

Colours and lettering (or *typeface*) give out strong messages that will tell your potential customers a lot about you. There are endless shades and combinations of colours that give different impressions (for example, khaki green sends a very different message from deep sea green), but here is a general guide to the hidden messages of colour:

63

- red is a dynamic colour, better for selling cars than yoga classes
- blue is soothing, especially lighter shades (you could use this for the yoga classes)
- deep, rich colours (burgundy, royal blue and so on) imply opulence and quality, but they can appear old-fashioned
- browns and greens (especially in combination) give an impression of rustic simplicity – great for hand-knitted jumpers; not so good for photocopier accessories
- yellow is cheerful (not ideal for funeral directors)
- dayglo colours give a cheap and cheerful impression.

This is by no means an exhaustive list, but it gives you enough of an idea to form your own views when observing other people's logos. One other important point: if you export, check the meaning of your chosen colour in the countries you plan to export to.

White means death in Japan, for instance, and black and red are the colours associated with evil spirits in Brazil.

LETTERING

When it comes to lettering, once again look at other companies and products. See what the following typefaces suggest to you, and notice what different impressions they give.

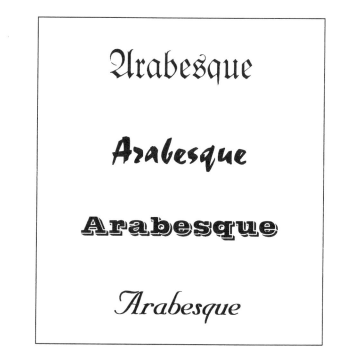

There are a couple of practical points to bear in mind as well when you're choosing a logo:

- the fewer colours you use, the cheaper it will be to print
- if you pick a standard typeface it will be easier and cheaper to recreate if you lose the artwork than an obscure or specially designed typeface; this is worth including in your brief to a

designer if you are using one. There are hundreds of typefaces available, so you can still choose a relatively unknown one if you want to

- if you're not a designer, the first rule of DIY logo design is *keep it simple.*

Let's have a look at Arabesque. What do you want to say to your customers? You could say useful, imaginative, high-quality, affordably priced, stylish. What is it that will bring customers to your door, though? Well, there are cheaper ways of training plants; people will use Arabesque because they care about the aesthetics – they want their gardens to look more attractive. So let's find a logo that says 'stylish'. How about this?

This is a useful typeface to use. It's called University Roman and most printers and high street print shops will have it, so we can always match it, whatever printer or designer we use.

Now, how about colour? This is a gardening product after all, so perhaps an earthy colour: brown or green. But if we want to look stylish it will need to be a classy shade of brown or green, not a folksy one. After looking at several shades of brown and green (in magazines, on book jackets, on food packets and anywhere else that catches your eye), let's say you choose a deep, rich, slightly terracotta shade of brown. It gives an impression of style and originality (it's an unusual colour), and it echoes the colour of soil and flower pots. And dark, rich colours usually have a traditional air about them – this is the kind of product (you imply) that wealthy Victorians would have put in their gardens if only they'd thought of it.

Stationery

Once you've chosen your logo (the printer can actually draw it up if you tell them exactly what you want), the next thing you'll want to sort out will be stationery. First of all, you need to decide where to put the logo. People often put it in the top left-hand corner, or the centre, without noticing that there are alternatives. Without a designer, you need to consider the options for yourself.

Take into account the design of the logo itself. Some designs ask to be in a left- or right-hand corner. A central logo, with white space on either side, often has a clean simplicity that is very classy. Some companies put the logo down the side, or at the bottom of the page, or diagonally across a corner. These can look rather stilted, of course, if there isn't a reason for it, but can be very effective if there is. For example, if you run a company called Down Under that sells traditional Australian artifacts, it could be very catchy to put your logo at the bottom of the page.

In the case of Arabesque, we want to promote the simple, stylish look. So let's put the logo at the top of the letterhead, in the centre, and drop the address and other details to the bottom of the page. This will emphasise the clean, elegant lines of the logo, which will suggest that the product has the same attributes.

PAPER

The paper you use says a lot about you. Try looking at other companies' choices of paper and notice the variety that's available. The difference in price between thin, flimsy typing paper and a slightly heavier letterhead paper is not that great, and if you want to give an impression of quality, this is not the place to economise. But avoid fancy papers like parchment style or marbled papers as these are expensive.

If you want to use coloured paper, follow the same guidelines as before about the messages different colours send to your customers. Consider as well:

- when you type or print on to darker papers, the text could be harder to read

- coloured papers look darker once they have been typed on. Even if you don't think the colour is very deep, it could look drab, especially next to the brightly coloured glossy brochure you send with it

- once you start to use a coloured paper you will need to be consistent with it, which means that every time you use the colour on brochures, exhibition panels and so on, it will need to match the letterhead. So make sure you pick a colour that is easy to duplicate on glossy brochure paper or stick-on vinyl lettering for the shop window. (You'll never be able to match *everything*, but you'll get closer with ivory, say, than you will with an unusual shade of pale salmony peach.)

KEEP YOUR STYLE CONSISTENT

One of the most important single factors in producing printed material is consistency. Make sure that everything you produce follows the same style. Delivery notes, labels, invoices and statements should be printed in the same colour as the letterheads, with the logo in the same position. Everything your customers see should give the same message.

THINK BEFORE YOU PRINT

Don't print more than you need. We'll look at getting quotes from printers later in this chapter, but, apart from the amount of stationery you stockpile, consider the number of formats you need. Some companies have A4 and A5 (that's half A4 size) letterheads. This can be quite handy for writing short letters, but check what it will cost. Not that much, admittedly, but is it really worth it? On a low budget, every little counts. Consider a couple of non-standard options:

- you could print your compliment slips on A5 paper (a bit bigger than standard), which could double as A5 letter paper for your short letters

- if you print standard compliment slips in portrait format (tall and thin) this can give you more room for writing messages.

Some companies have half a dozen stationery items, before you include invoices and delivery notes. The less you need to use, the less you have to pay, so double up what you can.

BUSINESS CARDS

It's worth singling out business cards from the rest of your stationery, as they have a special marketing significance. It is a fact that people are far more likely to keep your business card than your compliment slip, or even a letter. People keep business cards. They keep them in wallets and in old tissue boxes on their desks. And every time they look through them (to find the number of that person who prints names on biros, who handed them a card at an exhibition last year) they see every other card in the box, including yours. Next time a friend says that the summer jasmine is looking a mess, they'll say, 'There's a company that makes unusual frames for training plants over – they look really smart. I'll dig their name out for you.'

It's worth printing business cards from the start. Print them on good quality card (it doesn't have to cost a lot) and clip one on to every letter you send out. The letter may go in the bin, but the card will most likely be kept or passed on to someone who could use your product or service. The sooner you run out of business cards and have to reorder, the more pleased you should be with yourself. Business cards are one of the cheapest and most effective forms of advertising.

It's often worth printing some business cards with no name on them. When you take on new staff, you don't necessarily want to pay to print business cards just for them – much more economical to wait a few weeks until you're paying for another job at the printer's at the same time. In the meantime, the new person doesn't have to go without – they can write in their name by hand on a blank card.

BORDER PAPER

Here's another piece of stationery you may find handy. As well as plain continuation sheets, think about having some sheets printed with a simple design in your corporate colour around the

edges only (not necessarily all round, but not spilling onto the main area of the page).

Next time you produce a photocopied price list, programme for a PR event you're holding, information sheet for your customers or whatever, put this paper in the photocopier instead of plain paper. Hey presto, a smart, two-colour sheet instead of a plain old photocopy. If you don't want to pay for special press release paper (with 'press release' printed on it in big letters) this will do, with the words 'press release' typed large at the top.

Writing your own material

You can pay agencies and freelances to write your brochures and catalogues for you – and it won't be cheap. Once again, if you want a job done cheaply, do it yourself. Many people are terrified of writing their own material, but it's really not that hard if you approach the task methodically.

The very first thing to do is to decide what it is you need to print. One of the easiest ways to waste money is to produce something that costs more than it earns. We might start off assuming that in order to sell Arabesque climbing frames we need a brochure to send out. But let's think about it for a moment first.

WHO ARE OUR POTENTIAL CUSTOMERS?

Well, there are all the gardeners who want to tidy up their climbing plants or create decorative fencing. Then there are the companies who want to landscape their car parks and grounds. And councils and municipal parks who might buy them in large quantities, and might want us to erect them. Then there are the garden centres, garden designers and landscape gardeners who can sell the frames on to their customers.

Are they all looking for the same benefits?

■ The gardeners probably aren't too price-sensitive (or they'd be looking at cheaper products in the first place). But they need to know how easy the frames are to erect, and to be reassured about how wonderful they'll look when they're up.

■ Businesses and councils are likely to be working to tight budgets; they want something that looks smart and lasts, but they need to be able to justify the cost. They'll be concerned about the amount of maintenance the plants will need if they use these frames. They'd want us to erect them, too, but we can't afford to offer this service to individual customers.

■ The garden centres and designers want to be able to sell to customers in our first category – private gardeners – but they'd buy at a discount. They want to know that *their* customers will be satisfied. And the designers will want to know that the frames are easy to erect – time is money and they don't want to spend all day putting up half a dozen frames.

So it looks as if we need two brochures. We can use the same one for the private gardeners, garden centres and designers, as long as we print two price lists and send trade prices to the garden centres and designers. But we definitely need to say something slightly different to businesses and public authorities, so we'd better print a slightly different brochure for them, with more emphasis on how simple the frames are to maintain, and plenty of facts to justify the cost. And we should also tell them that we can erect the frames for them.

71

You need to go through this thought process whenever you print a new leaflet, catalogue or whatever. Otherwise you could be sending potential customers brochures that don't explain what *they* want to know.

BENEFITS NOT FEATURES

Always think of what your customers want in terms of benefits, not features. Don't think of what the product does, but what it does *for the customer*. In other words, one of the features of an Intercity train is that it travels very fast, but the benefit is that you arrive at your destination sooner. A feature of Arabesque frames is that they are made of plastic-coated aluminium tubing;

the benefits are that they aren't heavy to move around and they last for years without breaking or rusting.

This is the key to deciding what written material to produce, and how many brochures you need. You could have 20 distinct types of customer, but if they are all interested in the same benefits, you may well only need a single brochure. Or, as with Arabesque, only three or four types of customer could still need more than one brochure between them.

WHAT ARE YOU TRYING TO ACHIEVE?

Why are you producing this brochure, catalogue, exhibition display or whatever it is? You need to identify your objective before you pick up your pen. Do you want the customer to telephone you and say, 'I'd like to order 25 of these, please'? Or do you want them to say, 'Can you send me some more information?' or 'I'd like you to come and have a look at our car park and give us a quotation'?

Defining your objective is important because it will determine what you say. If you want them to ask for more information, you'd better not tell them everything in your leaflet (for a high price item you might never sell direct from an unsolicited leaflet, your best bet is to encourage them to make contact so you can follow up later). If you want them to ask for a quote, you'd better say 'phone us for a quotation'.

It may sound obvious, but it's very easy to find yourself writing about the product in a general sort of way without really knowing why you're doing it. The effect is often transmitted to the reader – 'It looks quite interesting, but what am I supposed to do about it? Rush out and buy one? Wait for them to call?' If you are focused on your objective, the customer will be able to focus on it more easily, too.

MAKE IT READABLE

Plan out what needs saying before you start to write, and resist the temptation to write too much. If there are only five things that will affect the reader's decision to buy, call for a quote or what-

72

ever, only say those five things. If there is a lot to say, break it into sections with headings and subheadings, use bullet points, or put some information in a separate box ('how to order', perhaps, or 'plants to use with Arabesque frames').

THINK LIKE A CUSTOMER

While you are writing, or when you read back what you've written, try to imagine you're a potential customer reading the brochure and ask yourself the following questions.

- Do the benefits sound worthwhile?
- Is there any jargon that you wouldn't understand as a customer?
- Is there anything missing that you would want to know?
- Is the style credible? If you've written 'The incredible Arabesque climbing frame will amaze you. It will transform your garden overnight; you won't believe it . . .' . . . they probably won't believe it. It may work for some products, but not for many. The usual reaction to this approach is 'They would say that, wouldn't they?'

73

Ask somebody else (as many people as you like, in fact) to read over what you've written. Ask them to try to think like a customer too, and to be as critical as they like – it's worth it. Think of the sales you could lose because your friends were too polite to tell you that your brochure wasn't convincing enough.

WRITING PLAIN ENGLISH

There are whole books on how to write clearly. Essentially, though, the best approach is to write as you speak:

- avoid the most obvious slang, but otherwise use a chatty, friendly style
- avoid jargon. What is jargon to one person is everyday speech to another, so remember to judge what is or isn't jargon from the customer's point of view

- write in the second person; as soon as you address the reader as 'you' they feel more involved

- use short words, sentences and paragraphs

- use active, not passive, verbs. In other words don't say, 'If you would like to be advised by us', say, 'If you would like us to advise you'; rather than 'Arabesque frames can be erected in under five minutes', say, 'You can erect Arabesque frames . . .'

- avoid abstract nouns. They're all the ones that end -tion, -ity and so on. Don't say 'Transportation of the frames will be provided', say, 'We will deliver the frames'.

BE PRACTICAL

Some companies print lots of glossy brochures and end up throwing half of them away. Why? Because the prices have gone out of date. We low cost marketeers can't afford to do that, so try to avoid printing prices, dates, names of personnel or anything else that could change before you're ready to reprint the brochures. You can always print a separate leaflet or price list, which is cheaper to produce, and you can print fewer of them. If you really can't avoid putting your prices in your brochure, at least consider ordering fewer of them in the first place.

And finally, see if you can spot the deliberate mistake in this leaflet.

The Golden Lion

Alan and Jennifer
Welcome you to our

HISTORIC VILLAGE INN
0803-123456

Accommodation
Excellent Food
Parties Catered For

Ideal for a stop-off point or use as a base for touring the South West

Where is it? No, not the mistake, the pub? We all have off days, and even the smartest of us make mistakes at times, but when you're trying to save money you've got to get it right first time, and you can't afford to send out 5000 leaflets on which you forgot to put your address. So here's a checklist of the practical details that can so easily be left off brochures, leaflets and any other printed material. They don't have to be printed large – they're the sort of details that people will look for if they want them – but they need to be there. Remember to include:

- address
- phone number
- contact names
- who to make the cheque payable to
- price
- page numbers (if you refer to them in a contents list or index, for a catalogue or annual report)
- venue (for events)
- date (for events)
- closing date.

75

Getting the best from your printer

Once you have written your material, there are three basic stages it must go through:

1 *Design* deciding what the text and illustrations will look like, where they will go, what typefaces, colours and so on to use
2 *Typesetting and artwork* actually doing the design work once these decisions have been made, typesetting the text and then positioning it on the page, along with any illustrations. At the end of this process you have what is known as 'camera-ready artwork', that is, artwork that is ready for the printers to go ahead without any corrections, additions or changes.

3 *Printing.*

There are three options as to who can do this work:

1 *a designer* (who may be freelance or work in-house for the printer) would normally design, typeset and prepare the artwork. You would need to give them an outline brief
2 *a printer* could do the typesetting and prepare the artwork if you are not using a designer. They will obviously do the printing, whoever does the rest of the work
3 *You* can prepare an outline brief for a designer, or a detailed design brief to pass on to the printer for typesetting. If you have a desktop publishing (DTP) software package you could typeset the text, and maybe prepare camera-ready artwork, as well.

There are obviously a lot of permutations here, and the key factor in deciding which option to choose is money. As usual, the more you do yourself, the less you will have to pay anybody else. If you don't have DTP facilities, you will have to pay someone else for the typesetting and artwork. If the job is small and simple (such as a business card when you already have your logo designed), and you have a good eye for design, brief the printer to do it. If the job is complex, vitally important (a 50-page catalogue for your biggest mailshot yet) and you can't tell a Rembrandt from a five-year-old's scribble, brief a designer.

Most jobs will fall somewhere between these two extremes; the only answer is to get quotes, and then find the best balance between what you can afford, what each option will cost, and how much design input you think is needed.

THE ROUTE THROUGH THE PROCESS

So you've decided to produce a brochure for gardeners, garden centres and garden designers. You know what you want to say – which benefits you're going to emphasise. Now what happens? We'll look at each of these stages in more detail later in this chapter, but here's an overview of getting material printed, from start to finish.

1 The first thing is to decide on the outline design. How many pages? What size? What colours? (Printers think black is a colour, by the way.) Will you use illustrations? What sort? What kind of paper do you want to print on?

2 Once you have this information, you are ready to get quotes, work out the cost, change anything that turns out to be unaffordable and decide who to give the work to.

3 Once you have decided on the details of the job and who will be doing it, *tell the printer*. If the printer is not involved at an earlier stage, this often gets forgotten until the artwork is ready, which is not the time to find out that the paper you want must be ordered three weeks ahead.

4 Now give the brief to the designer, or a more detailed brief to the typesetter if you're not using a designer. If you have decided to do the typesetting and artwork yourself, you're ready to get started.

5 You should get two or three sets of proofs from whoever is doing the typesetting and artwork. You will need to check these and return them.

6 Once you have returned the final proof, the printer will get on and print the job.

THE OUTLINE DESIGN

You need to make certain decisions, which will affect the final cost, before you can ask for quotes. This is also a useful process to go through to be absolutely clear what impression you want to give your potential customers. Many people are unaware of just how many subliminal messages we send out by our choice of paper, colour, typeface and so on.

At this stage we need to know the following:

1 pages
   ■ how many?
   ■ what size and shape?
2 paper (your printer may refer to it as 'stock')
   ■ weight?

- colour?
- finish?

3 colour
- how many colours?
- do you want to use tints?
- will you use colour on every page?

4 illustrations
- what type?
- photographs – colour, black and white, duotone or other?

Let's look at each of these aspects in detail.

Pages

Number

To a printer, pages are sides of paper. So a single sheet printed on both sides is two pages. Decide how many pages, as a printer understands the word, it will take to say everything you want to, and illustrate anything that calls for a drawing or photo. Bear in mind that any brochure will look more inviting and be easier to read if the text is comfortably spaced out, so don't try to cram everything into two pages if it could comfortably fill four.

Size

It's worth becoming familiar with the terms for standard paper sizes, if you don't already know them. A4 paper is the size you usually put through your printer or photocopier, and is the standard size for letterheaded paper. If you know this, you can work the rest out from here. A3 is twice A4, A2 is twice A3 (and so on up to A0). They always double into the fattest shape possible, so A3 is the shape of two A4 sheets laid side to side, not end to end. Half A4 is A5, and half A5 is A6.

If you want a brochure with a fold in the middle, you'll need to specify both the original and the eventual size of the paper (this avoids any possible misunderstandings). For our Arabesque brochure, let's say we need four sides of A4 to say everything we want to without cramping it. So we specify A3, folded to make four

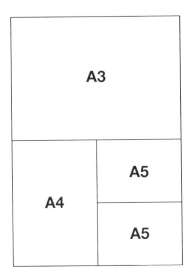

pages of A4. Or, in printers' jargon, 'A3 folded to A4'.

Shape

The other thing you need to decide is the shape of the page – whether you want your A4 pages to be in portrait format (taller than they are wide) or landscape format (wider than they are tall).

Paper

The paper (or card) you choose will have a huge effect on the impression you make. Chunky or flimsy, glossy or matt, people will judge your product or service by the 'stock' you use. Pick up all the leaflets, magazines, letters, brochures and so on that you can find. Examine the different types of paper. You'll find that your local freebie magazine is probably printed on newsprint, while *Country Life* is printed on heavy gloss paper. What does that tell you about their comparative quality and the markets they are aiming at?

Weight

Paper is graded according to weight and measured in gsm (grammes per square metre). The thinner the paper, the less it weighs. A flimsy typing paper might be 70 gsm; letterheads are most commonly printed on 100 gsm paper. You'll need to get a printer to show you samples and swatches of paper. For an outline brief, you can give a designer or printer a sample of something you've found that you like – don't worry if you don't actually know what weight it is. If you print on thin paper, the ink can show through on the other side. If you're worried about this, ask your printer's advice.

Colour

Do you want to print on coloured paper? Remember the points we covered earlier in this chapter about coloured letterheaded paper – it can be hard to match, it can look darker than you expect, and it can make the text harder to read. It may also change the appearance of any colour you print on top of it. Having said this, there are times when it works very well, and if you can't afford to print in a second colour of ink, you can use the paper to give the brochure a lift with another colour.

Finish

You can buy paper in several different finishes, and your designer or printer should be able to show you samples. The principal types of finish are bond (mostly used for stationery and simple leaflets), matt (an eggshell-type finish) and gloss. Surprisingly, matt paper often looks more expensive than glossy paper – it can give an appearance of understated quality.

Glossy paper can be very reflective, which makes it harder to read under bright lights. Heavy gloss paper, coupled with a sophisticated design, will look very smart, though. If you want to illustrate something shiny, like diamond jewellery, it would probably be the finish to choose.

Photographs work much better on a matt or gloss finish than bond. Some finishes, particularly some of the unusual ones, do not pick up the ink as well during the printing process. This is something you need to check with your printer if you are considering this kind of paper. However, most of these papers are very expensive and so are unlikely to be compatible with a low cost approach to printing.

Colour

Number of colours

You pay extra for every colour you use. This is because each sheet of paper has to go through the press once for each colour. If you only use one colour it doesn't really matter which you choose, although black will be a fraction cheaper (only because the printers probably won't have to 'wash up' their equipment – they use black so often, they'll put your job through next to another one that's printing in black already).

If you are printing chunks of text, they will be hard to read unless they are in black or another very dark colour. Most companies use their house colour or colours for headlines, drawings, twirly bits and so on, and black for the text. If your house colour is right, though, you can save money by using it for the text as well so you don't have to pay for the black ink. The best colours for this are very dark blues, greens, purples, reds and browns.

Tints

Another way to avoid paying for extra colours is to use a tint of one of the colours you are already printing. A tint is a lighter shade, and is expressed as a percentage of the original colour. So a 20% tint of dark blue has been diluted to 20% of its original strength, and will look like a light blue. You can then use both dark and light blue at far lower cost than printing two different colours (tints do cost a little extra though). A word of warning about tints: always ask the printer to show you a swatch of the tint before you use it – some of them can look dreadful, and you probably won't see the finished version until the job has been completed.

How many pages?

The printer can't print more than one sheet of paper at a time (which may subsequently be folded), and can only print on one side of the paper at once. Every sheet has to go through the press once for each colour. So one way to save money is to print certain colours only on some of the sheets. That way, the other sheets won't have to go through again.

Illustrations

What type?

Decide whether you will be using illustrations and, if so, what type. Line drawings? Sketches? Do they already exist or will you want the designer to draw them? How many do you want? Will people want to know how to erect Arabesque frames before they decide to buy them? Will you need a diagram to illustrate it? Do you need to illustrate all the available designs and, if so, should you use drawings or photographs?

Photographs

If you decide to use photographs, there is another cost decision to make. Colour photographs are very expensive to reproduce. If you don't have any decent black and white photographs, it may actually be cheaper to pay a professional photographer to take some specially than to print the colour photographs you've already got.

If you have a colour photograph with enough contrast, you may be able to reproduce it in black and white. The best way to see if it will work is to put it through a good quality photocopier. If the reds and greens have all turned into the same shade of grey, you could have a problem; but if you can still see the picture clearly you can probably print it in black and white without any difficulty.

Of course, there are times when colour photographs are worth it – in fact, some products virtually demand to be photographed in colour. But even if your budget can stretch to it, make it a rule never to include colour photographs in any printed material without at least asking yourself first whether you couldn't manage with black and white ones.

One other option for photographs, which is closer to the price of black and white than colour, is a duotone. Suppose you are printing in black and deep blue. If you print your photographs in duotone, the black will still be black and the white, white. But all the greys in between will be blue-grey. A printer should be able to show you examples and tell you how it will look using your colours (it's better with dark colours). It can give a very classy look at a lower cost than printing photographs in colour.

CHOOSING YOUR DESIGNER AND PRINTER

As far as both designers and printers are concerned, you need to ask around and get recommendations if you can. Ask to see examples of their work, and ask if you can talk to satisfied customers. Some designers and printers have better reputations than others for delivering on time – this is a point well worth checking on when you follow up their references.

Printers come in different sizes. Some of them can produce giant posters covered in colour photographs, print them on plastic, weatherproof sheeting and then cut them so they're shaped like elephants. Others can't print anything bigger than A3. You will almost invariably find that the printers who do the fancy stuff are more expensive. They've got to pay off the loans they took out to buy all their clever machines. If all you want is a single sheet of A3 printed in black, go to the printer that can't do anything more. The only exception to this is if you're printing large quantities, as a bigger outfit can probably get a better deal from the paper manufacturer.

The general rule is: use the smallest set-up that can do what you want. This may well mean that, if you do a lot of printing, you may have two or three regular printers – many companies do. So you use the local jobbing printer for your stationery; for the colour brochures and catalogues you go somewhere else; and you use a really expensive printer for the annual report and the exhibition displays, because nobody else can do them.

It's also worth mentioning that there are one or two incredibly cheap print companies around that keep their costs down by printing in bulk for numerous customers at a time. These are worth checking out, but usually the costs are low because your options (typefaces, colour, stock and so on) are limited. Don't compromise your quality, style, corporate image or design integrity – it's not worth it. But if they supply what you want, go for it.

WHAT'S IT GOING TO COST?

Budget

Now here's something surprisingly few people do – set a budget *before* you ask for quotations. Otherwise how will you know whether to say yes or no to the price? The most sensible way to work out what a brochure, exhibition display or whatever is worth is to work out how much money it is likely to earn you, directly or indirectly. If we're going to put 1000 leaflets around local garden centres, how many sales do we expect to make, at what profit?

Deduct from this profit the cost of the time you spend working on the brochure, the cost of mailing it, and so on. What is left has to cover design, printing, and your final profit from the whole exercise.

Now you know how much money you have (or haven't) got to play with, it's time to get some prices. Ask at least three designers (if you're using a designer) and printers to give you quotes so you can compare – prices can vary enormously. As a typical example, three quotes I was given for one particular job, by three reputable printers, ranged from around £900 to £1200.

Print run

In addition to the information you have put together for the outline design brief, you will need to supply one or two other pieces of information. The printer will need to know how many copies of the brochure you need, which they will call the size of the print run. You may not be sure; it might be affected by the cost. So your best bet is to ask for two separate prices – the basic run, and the 'run on' cost. The basic price eats up all the fixed costs – typesetting, making plates (the term for the 'negatives' from which the pages are printed), scanning illustrations and everything else – and the unit price then drops dramatically. The run on price is the cost of printing extra copies, which only carry the variable costs – paper, ink, machine time and so on.

If you know you want at least 1000 brochures, but you'd like up to

2000 if you could afford it, ask the printers to quote for 1000 and for a 500 run on. If the first 1000 will cost £600, every subsequent 500 may only cost, say, £145.

Finishing

Your printing will come off the press in flat sheets, which the printer will cut to size. If you want them to do anything else, such as fold or staple, you will need to tell them now so they can build the cost of it into their quote.

Give everyone the same brief

You can't compare prices unless you have given everyone the same brief. Suppose the second printer you speak to says, 'Why don't you drop the second colour on the inside pages, that will save a bit?' You reply, 'That's a good idea – yes, quote for that please.' Then the next printer says, 'I've just got a sample of some new paper. It's only a little bit more expensive, and it'll make a huge difference to the quality. Shall I price for using it?' You look at the paper and decide it is better, so you ask them to go ahead and quote for it.

The next week, three quotes arrive on your desk. Which is cheapest? The first printer's is a bit higher than the second, but then they quoted for two colours throughout. The third is a bit higher too, but it includes the nicer paper. You realise that you've just wasted everyone's time, including your own, and you have to go back and get at least two of them to quote again.

If a printer suggests an alternative to you – and the good ones often will – say, 'That's a good idea, please give me a quote for it. But please give me a quote for the original specification as well.'

Timescale

When you ask for a quote, state the deadline and ask the designer or printer to let you know what date they would need to start on it to meet it. Give the printer the delivery date (to be safe, tell them you need it a couple of days before you really do), and if you are using a designer, make their deadline for having the artwork ready the date by which the printer needs it.

Printers need much longer than you might imagine to do a job. They have to order the paper in advance, maybe typeset the text, wait while you check the proofs, put in the corrections, deal with the illustrations and photographs, lay tints, make plates, print, cut, fold, staple – and fit it all in with their commitments to their other customers.

It's safe to assume that the very simplest job you could devise would take a week, unless you had booked it in and agreed the schedule with them well in advance. By the way, it's worth noting that printers are usually particularly busy in the lead up to Christmas. However, a lot of printers have other busy times determined by, for example, an 80-page magazine they print once every three months.

Be considerate to your printer

Planning and scheduling is a major part of a printer's job. As a result, many printers are understandably prone to raise their prices to customers who frequently mess up their system. If you are unwise enough to earn a reputation for getting printers to redo quotes because you've changed the specification, asking for rush jobs, or changing things at the last minute any printer with sense will build a contingency cost into their quotes. So simply treating your printer with consideration will help you to keep your costs down.

Specification checklist

Here is a quick checklist of the details to include in your specification when you're asking for quotes; you could use it to create your own standard quotation request form:

- reference number/title of job
- print run (number)

- quote for run on (number)
- pages
  number:
  size:
  format:
- paper
  weight:
  colour:
  finish:
- colour
  number of colours:
  number of pages of additional colour:
  tints:
- illustrations
  number:
  style:
- photographs
  number:
  black and white/colour:
- finishing
- deadline
  please state when you would need copy/camera-ready artwork

Trimming the price down

So you budgeted £2500 and the best quote is £2950. What can you do? The important thing is to find ways of cutting the cost without cutting the quality. And there are plenty of options. They may not all be viable, but you usually find there's enough scope to trim the costs somewhere.

Number

Obviously the fewer copies you print, the less it will cost. But there are two things to bear in mind. First, it's only those variable costs you save – the bulk of the print bill will remain intact. And second, don't lose sight of the original object of the exercise. If you worked out what your expected income was from this exercise, cutting the print run is likely to reduce that income. It could be better to economise elsewhere.

Size

This is usually a solution when you need to reduce the cost dramatically. You could rethink your 20-page annual report, making it a 12-page annual report.

Stock

First of all, check with your printer. There may be another paper manufacturer who makes an almost identical paper to the one you chose, but at a better price – it often happens. Ask the printer or designer to find you the closest match they can. It's almost always a bad idea to switch from, say, 135 gsm (a nice, thick paper) to 100 gsm. It will look cheaper and tackier than the impression you had planned to give. However, it may be that a similar but different finish will reduce the price. Or the colour you wanted is only made by one, expensive company, and a change of colour would mean you could switch to a manufacturer whose product is more reasonably priced.

Colour

This is a popular place to save money. If you drop from three colours to two, your potential customers won't know you ever meant to do anything else. Of course, you'll know that the third colour would have been the icing on the cake, but your design and choice of stock will still imply the same quality. You may even save more money than you need to, and what you have in hand might pay for you to use tints you hadn't previously budgeted for.

You may find that you don't have to drop one colour completely, just use it on only some of the sheets. It's the printer's plates you're paying for. Their press might print A3 paper (which they'll cut down later if you've ordered an A5 booklet, for instance). This means that they work in terms of A3 plates. Your annual report is 20 A4 pages, and there are two A4 pages to an A3 plate, so that's ten plates. How about using your second colour on only five of them?

There are other variations on this theme, such as keeping one colour throughout and then using your other two colours on alternate plates instead of using them both right through. Your printer may even find a way to do you a favour: if they hold your job up until they're printing something in the same colour for another customer, they could let you off paying for washing up the equipment (this is strictly a favour, mind you – don't expect it of them).

Illustrations
The best way to save money here is to use fewer of them. However, if you're illustrating how to erect Arabesque, for example, make sure the instructions are still clear. This is not a sensible economy if the meaning of the brochure loses its clarity.

Could you reduce the number of photographs, or change them from colour to duotone or black and white? If you can do this without too much damage, the space you might save could mean you can also reduce the number of pages.

89

Finishing
Be wary of trying to save money here. If you were planning to stitch your booklet, you could decide to staple it instead, or change to a less expensive form of binding. However, many people are tempted to save a few pounds by doing their own folding. This usually saves very little, unless you are printing a huge number of copies. And in that case it will take you forever to fold them. If you are thinking of it, though, remember to take into account the cost of your own time – after all, you could have spent the time chasing sales leads. Is it really profitable to spend half a day folding leaflets yourself in order to save a tenner?

Offcuts
Suppose your printer has an A3 press. You are printing an unusual size of brochure – it's A4 width, but only two thirds of the height. Think about how the printer will fit it on the press. The top third of the plate will be empty so, after it's gone through the press, it will become an offcut.

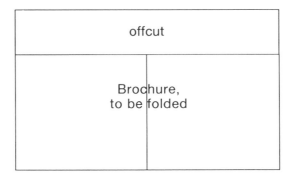

If you can come up with something useful to print in this top third, it will cost almost nothing – you're already paying for the plate, the time on the press, the colour, the cutting. The only additional costs will be a bit of extra designing and typesetting. Keep it simple and this should be a very small charge. The final bill won't be less, but you'll get more for your money, and save the budget you would have allocated to the additional part of the work if you'd printed it separately.

What can you do with the extra space? It depends first of all on the stock you're using, and the size and shape of the offcut. After these considerations, you're limited only by your imagination. Do you need more business cards? Name badges? Could you use name cards for conferences or training sessions – the type you fold in half lengthwise and stand on the desk? Or free giveaways for your customers – a calendar for the noticeboard? Something appropriate to your business – a bookmark, a reminder card of important exhibition dates, an instruction reminder card for how to use your equipment? There's usually something once you think about it.

Running jobs together

This should be obvious, but it is often ignored. If you hold on to non-urgent print jobs until you have other printing to do, the cost will be lower than doing them separately. The printer will put everything in the same colour through at once, so you only have to pay for cleaning the equipment once. As we know, one of the primary rules of low cost marketing is to think. We can't afford to waste money by not planning ahead.

Mailing costs

If you're going to mail out your leaflets, annual reports or whatever they are, check what this will cost you in terms of:

■ envelopes

■ postage.

Do you need to save a lot on this bill? If you changed the format, you might be able to use smaller envelopes. Alternatively, you could fold the contents – mind you, anything printed on heavy paper will look bad folded, as will anything that is stapled, or intended to look very smart. But leaflets or small brochures can still look fine, especially if you design them to look as though they were always meant to be folded.

If you could reduce the weight of the mailshot, you might drop into a lower band of postage. You could do this in a number of ways:

■ use a thinner paper (don't compromise the quality, but cutting down from card to heavy paper, say, could still look very smart)

■ print on smaller pages. Reduce the amount to go on the page by losing a little bit of the blank space on the page if you can spare it, use a slightly smaller size of print (but only *slightly*), sneak the size of the illustrations down a fraction, or a combination of these techniques. This does work, but do be careful, don't cramp the text up too much

■ reduce the number of pages. This usually means cutting whole sections – you'll never be able to cut that much just by taking out the odd sentence here or there. Leave out all four pages on the history of the company in the annual report, for example, or the whole section on how to erect Arabesque frames in the brochure – a brief gist of what is involved will do for now, and you can send the details with the frames when they buy them. Or you could take out the 12-page price list and print it separately from the catalogue on much lighter paper.

91

Talk to the designer and printer

Ask for advice. A good designer or printer will be able to make useful suggestions. Take them seriously, but remember that even though their knowledge of the techniques may be greater than yours, you understand your business and your customers best. The printer will know how much money you can save by removing four pages from your brochure, but only you know whether potential customers will buy Arabesque frames without knowing exactly how to assemble them.

One of the most useful things you can do is to ask your printer to spend an hour or two showing you round and explaining the printing process to you. You will identify all sorts of useful tips, understand why some things work out cheaper than others, and realise why printers need the time they do for each job, once you see it all in action. You will find it time well spent.

How *not* to save money

Before we leave the subject of keeping costs down, it's worth mentioning some 'economies' to avoid:

- it is almost never a good idea to buy the paper direct from the manufacturer (to save the printer's mark-up). Some ink may not take on some paper, in which case who can you blame but yourself? The printer and manufacturer will each blame the other, or you for not checking. In any case, the printer will normally get a far better discount than you

- don't do anything yourself in order to save money – such as preparing illustrations, taking photographs, folding leaflets and so on – without costing your time and considering what else you could be doing instead

- beware of losing quality when you cut costs. Never lose sight of your original brief in terms of the level of quality you decided was necessary, and find economies that don't compromise this.

Designing your own material

If you are looking after the design – either doing it yourself or briefing the typesetter – there are certain basic guidelines to follow. DTP packages can be dangerous things. No-one assumes that just because you give them a gun, they can shoot accurately, but give them a DTP package and a PC and they instantly think they can design. Of course, a handful of them can, but I have seen far more leaflets and brochures ruined by DTP packages than improved by them.

Some people have a good eye for design, even if they are untrained, and others don't. If you don't, get someone else to do your design work. But use anyone you can get your hands on who does. If the most artistic person around is your receptionist or your business partner's 18-year-old son, ask them to do it for you. It'll be worth it for the difference they will make.

The single, most important rule is, once again, *keep it simple*.

93

White space

One of the most useful tools you have is 'white space' – just empty space with nothing printed on it at all. White space adds importance to whatever you put in the middle of it, and clean, simple lines give an air of style and quality.

There are times, however, when it is a good idea to look cluttered, but you still need simple lines so the reader knows where to find what they're looking for on the page. The busy, cluttered look implies a cheap and cheerful product range. If your strongest selling point is that your products are cheaper than your competitors', this look may be best for you. You'll find an example of both these approaches on the next page.

Typefaces and sizes

In order to be clear and uncluttered, avoid messing the page up with too many fonts. A font is a family of typefaces – the basic typeface and the same one in bold, italic, capitals and so on. Here is a useful rule of thumb for designing: never use more than two fonts to a page or double-page spread.

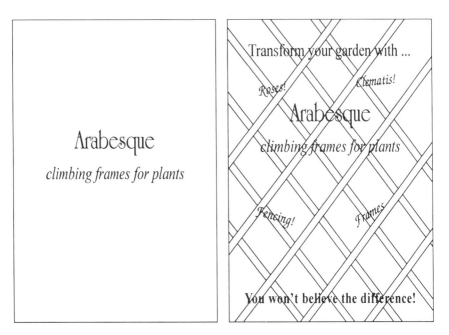

The design on the left, with plenty of white space, looks much classier.

Always print large chunks of text in a serif typeface; they're easier to read. Serif typefaces have twiddly bits on them, while *sans serif* ones don't.

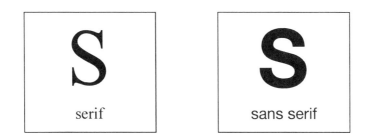

Don't print more than a sentence at a time in italic, capital letters, or a pale colour on a dark background – all of these are difficult to read.

The point size of the lettering is the height of each letter; 72-point type is exactly 1 inch high. The 'leading' is the space between the bottom of one line and the bottom of the next. According to research, the easiest point size to read is 10-point text on 12-point leading (if the leading was the same as the text, the tops of the letters would touch the bottoms of the letters on the line above).

You can do anything you like with point sizes for headings, captions and so on, but try to keep the body text as close to 10 point as you can; text below about 7 point is extremely hard to read.

Boxes, rules and tints

Putting self-contained sections of text in boxes or drawing rules under sections is a useful technique for keeping the page clean and easy to follow. You can use tints inside the boxes, but keep them light if you are printing text over them, and don't use too many to a page (unless they are very neatly arranged) or it will start to look messy.

PROOFS

You may get two or three sets of proofs from the typesetter. It is your responsibility to correct them. There are three main points to remember about proofreading:

- it is almost impossible to proof your own writing accurately, so get someone else to do it, and ask them to check the proofs against the originals, especially for phone numbers and other important details. You can't afford to reprint if you make a mistake, so the proofreading must be thorough.

- if there is a mistake in the final, printed version and this was also in the proofs (but you missed it), the responsibility lies with you, not the printer. They will not bear the cost of a reprint, so once again, don't let it happen.

- when you return the proofs, the printer will charge you extra for what are called 'author's corrections'. These are not typing errors, spelling mistakes and so on, but changes you make because you decide to rewrite that sentence, or switch those two paragraphs around because you think it might sound better.

This includes changes to typeface, style or layout if you originally left these to the printer's judgement. If you can't afford to pay, don't make the changes. Make sure that your final draft really is final before you hand it over to the typesetter.

DON'T GET CAUGHT OUT

Finally, here are a handful of legal considerations to bear in mind:

- when the job is finished, ask the printer to let you have the artwork back. You should make sure you retain ownership of it, and you might need it in future if you want to reprint, perhaps using a different printer

- get everything in writing (specifications, quotations and so on). Things will go wrong sooner or later and, if you believe it is the printer's fault, and you want them to pay for it to be put right, you'd better be able to prove that you asked for 10 000 copies and not 1000, or that delivery was due on the 5th, not the 15th

- you may not receive the exact quantity you ordered; a standard printer's contract is conditional on a margin of 5 or 10%, depending on the number of times the job goes through the press (less for print runs of over 50 000). Printers virtually never deliver short numbers in fact, but if you order 1000 colour brochures and only 900 turn up, you've got no legal grounds for complaint.

5

Public relations

If you want a job done properly, do it yourself

Public Relations, or PR, is all about building and sustaining a good relationship with the public. This covers not only your customers but also your suppliers, the local community and anyone else you deal with as an organisation. PR does not generate income directly, and many organisations on a tight budget are, therefore, tempted to avoid it. But there are four very good reasons for directing some of your efforts into PR:

■ it can, indirectly, have a considerable impact on income

■ you can use a lot of PR on a small or even non-existent budget

■ it can be a very effective way of getting advertising for nothing

■ mentions on the editorial pages have been measured as having a much higher impact than mentions in advertisements.

Good PR should strengthen your corporate image – it should give your public a clear understanding of who you are and what you do. In other words, it should publicise your company. There are four main ways of achieving this:

1 local, national and trade press
2 radio
3 television
4 non-media PR.

This chapter will look at how to make the most of these. But first of all, you need to be clear about the image you are trying to promote.

Corporate image

Companies are like people; they have personalities. One classic image test for your company is to ask yourself, 'If we were a car, what car would we be?' Most people think of Jaguar cars as exciting and daring, Volvos as reliable and safe, and Rolls-Royce as aristocratic. These are human character traits, but we apply them to companies. Plenty of organisations have negative traits – many of the utility companies, for example, are seen as uncaring. Bulldozers.

Your company has a personality. You can't help it. But you can make sure it's a personality you want it to have. It's easier when your business is new, or new to a particular market; once people have formed an image of you it's very hard to change it. One company that has managed it is Tesco. They used to have a cheap and cheerful, never-mind-the-quality-look-at-the-price image. Now they're seen as a modern, caring business that sells high quality products at a good price. It took them several years to change the public's perception of the company, and cost them more money than you or I even want to think about. We'll stick to the low cost approach if we can – getting it right first time.

We looked at corporate identity in the last chapter – it's vital that every piece of stationery or packaging, every invoice and every van in the fleet should present the same identity. And your logo, style and colours will play a large part in creating your corporate image. But there's more to it than that.

Every single contact that any customer or member of the public has with any of your employees should reinforce your image. So should every contact with any of your ex-employees, or your customers. And every visit to any of your buildings.

Here are a couple of illustrations of this point:

- it's very hard to convince your customers that you're a bright, modern company if every time they visit your office it's dirty and old-fashioned

■ the public won't see you as friendly and caring if there are people out there saying, 'I had a job interview there once, and they never even bothered to write and tell me I hadn't got the job.'

What you're aiming for is a strong, consistent image, because that's the most memorable kind. And the more easily your customers can remember and recognise you, the better. How many people buy Colman's mustard because it's actually better than the other brands, and how many have never even tried the other brands, because to them mustard *means* Colman's? That's what you're aiming for. Think of some other companies and brands with a strong, positive image, and think how different the images are: Marks & Spencer, Ovaltine, the Red Cross, Coca-Cola.

Whenever you publicise your organisation, remember the qualities you want to be known for. If you already have a positive image with your customers, play to it. But make sure everything you do backs it up – not just your printed materials, but also the way you answer the phone, the way your service engineers dress, the way you treat your staff and everything else. This is all part of PR, and if you don't do it, you will be rowing upstream against a current of your own making in all your public events and media relations. Hardly a cost effective way to channel your limited resources. So make sure that everyone in the company is pulling in the same direction in everything they do.

99

Getting in the papers

Editorial coverage in the papers can be worth far more than advertising, and costs virtually nothing. On average, five times as many people read editorials as advertisements. Whether it's trade journals and magazines, local or national papers, or radio or television, this kind of coverage is about the most cost effective publicity you'll ever find.

All you have to do is write a press release about your company, send it to the papers and they print it for free. Well, all right, it doesn't always seem that easy, but only because everyone else is doing it as well, and there's only so much space in each publication. So you just have to make sure that the editor thinks your article is more worthy of inclusion than the others. The first part of this chapter is about how to ensure exactly that.

GETTING IN WITH JOURNALISTS

You need to cultivate all the useful journalists you can. The better they know you, the more likely they are to remember the press releases you send them, answer your phone calls or ask you to comment on a story about your industry. Don't forget either that if you know a journalist in the trade press in your industry, they might be able to give you information for research purposes, so they're well worth cultivating. Follow low cost marketing rule two: *talk*. It costs nothing to meet and talk to journalists, and the value in terms of free publicity can be huge.

- *Identify the right person* The editor is probably too distanced from actual stories to be useful to you. You are likely to want the news or features editor, or the reporter or editor who covers your subject (gardening, business, leisure or whatever). Call them – the switchboard will tell you the name and put you through.

- *Arrange to meet them* Explain who you are and, if it's possible, ask them to come to your office for coffee or meet in a pub over lunch.

- *Ask for their help* Stories are the lifeblood of a journalist. They want you to become a good source, so they will be happy to tell you what kind of stories they want, which days to send them in, when their deadlines are and so on.

- *Tell them about your business* Let them know the basics – why you want publicity and what kind of message you want to put across. Give them a press pack (we'll look at what goes into this in a moment) and answer any questions they want to ask you.

- *Offer to be a spokesperson* Could you give them quotes or briefings to accompany stories they cover that are in your area? If you make caving equipment, could you (or someone in the company) contribute to local stories about caving accidents? Or could you write a monthly column on gardening? Don't do this unless you're sure of your facts, however, as the publicity you get if you're caught out won't do you any favours.

- *Talk about your ideas* Discuss any news stories you have, or ideas for features, and get them to tell you if you're on the right lines. Once they've pointed you in the right direction, it's hard for them not to cover the story.

If you're trying to cultivate the local press, you could hold a press party (if you're lucky enough to be based in London, you may be able to round up enough trade journalists to do this). Fix up a buffet lunch and some wine, and invite the press along. If you do this annually, particularly around Christmas time, you don't need to tag it on to any special event; just use it as a chance to thank the press for their support over the last year. Have plenty of company representatives there to chat to the journalists. It has a surprisingly beneficial effect – it's much easier to talk to someone on the phone once you've met them face-to-face, for example. It improves your relationship with the local press and their coverage of your company as well.

The press list

One of the most important things to do is to compile a press list, or possibly several. You want a ready list of everyone you send press releases to. Depending on your business, you may have more than one list; you could have a list of local press, and one or more trade press lists. Arabesque, for example, should probably have trade press lists for gardening magazines, the gardening trade (landscapers, garden centres and so on) and local government purchasing. Some press releases will go to everyone, but most will be rephrased for each sector; some will go to one or two lists only.

Several organisations publish directories of media contacts. Some of them include details of which special features will appear in each magazine over the next few months. *Editors* is updated quarterly, *PIMS Media Directories* are monthly and *Two Ten Communications* is published every two months (your nearest main library should have them).

Putting together a press pack

Assemble all the useful information about your company that you can, and produce a press pack for all your regular press, radio and TV contacts. That way, every time you publicise a new story, they already have half the information to hand. Update your press pack regularly, and always have copies available at press events. The pack should contain:

- your latest press release
- a 'backgrounder': a long press release that doesn't go out of date fast. It could be, for example, about the latest trends in your industry and how your company is responding to them
- a fact sheet – a brief history of the company, your latest figures, number of staff and offices, most successful products/services and so on
- photographs – write full captions that explain and identify the photographs (even if they get separated from the rest of the press pack), and stick them on the backs of the prints. Supply black and white ones to papers that don't print in colour
- biographies – notes on senior personnel
- sales literature
- annual report.

WHAT MAKES A GOOD STORY?

The most important thing here is to follow rule one: *think*. In this case, think like a reader. Your 'customer' is the editor, but the editor will print whatever they think their readers want to read. The key thing is to talk to the editors and journalists themselves and ask them what they want to write stories about.

We are all inclined to find what we do more interesting than other people sometimes find it. Every time you think you have an interesting story, try to put yourself through the following process. First of all, imagine you are a typical reader of the publication in question. So if you want to send a release to the local paper, take off your business hat and put on your slobbing-on-the-sofa-with-your-feet-up hat. Now imagine that the press release is from some other company, one you've never heard of. Is it still as interesting as it was?

There are certain key ingredients that the press are more likely to find interesting. Of course the specialist trade press might well be interested if you find a new manufacturing process that means your gizmos can now be accurately sized to the nearest 0.4 mm instead of the previous 0.6 mm. But the local press won't be. In general, though, there are some common factors that make for more interesting stories:

- news (as opposed to feature articles) – events, announcements
- good news stories – opening of a new factory
- human interest – staff retiring after 45 years' service
- anything quirky or unusual
- anything involving children
- anything involving animals
- anything involving celebrities
- anything accompanied by a really eye-catching photograph.

The other popular ingredient, of course, is scandal or bad news – but you won't be including this in your press releases. See pages 118–22 for how to cope when it's thrust upon you.

GENERATING STORIES

If you don't think you have a promising story at the moment, you can always make one up. This doesn't mean telling lies; it just means generating the story yourself. For example:

- you can make any general information sound more newsy and immediate by prefacing your press release, 'Arabesque have just announced . . .'. It's perfectly true – this press release *is* the announcement
- you hold an event, say the opening of a new building, *in order* to invite the press along to it. Otherwise you'd just have started using the building without any fanfare

103

- you create an event, such as donating a prize at the local school sports day

- set up a publicity stunt that the media won't be able to resist – you don't need any excuse to do this. Find something relevant to your product or service; for example, if you're a health and safety consultancy you could bungee jump from Clifton suspension bridge.

It's a good idea to plan your press releases well in advance to make sure you get regular coverage in the press. Pin up a 'press planner chart' on the wall, and mark on it everything you can think of that you could hang a press release on – from the date your annual report is printed to the Chinese New Year (you could train a clematis of Chinese origin up Arabesque frames). If there are any gaps in the planner once you've done this, those are the times to organise events.

The publication of press releases follows the law of diminishing returns, however. If you send out one a year, it will almost certainly get printed (assuming the subject is interesting and it's well written). If you flood the media with your releases every day, they won't print them all – but they'll print a lot more than one a year. The one thing that's certain is that if you never send out press releases, they'll never be printed. Try sending out a press release every week. Discuss the topic at your weekly team meeting if you have one. Then if nothing is pre-planned on your chart, you can discuss ideas.

If you send out press releases once a week, you need to avoid the 'saturation point', where the papers feel they've printed your name too often. You can do this by using stories where your name is only secondary in the story, like the prize at the school sports day (where it is the sports day that is the main story).

HOW TO WRITE A PRESS RELEASE

80% of press releases end up in the journalist's rubbish bin. But a good press release is a journalist's dream. They're busy people, and if you can send them exactly what they need without them having to lift a finger, they are far more likely to print it.

Writing your own press releases saves a fortune in employing a PR agency. And there's no need to panic: this is not a talent, it's merely a skill, and anyone can learn it – you just need to know the formula to write to.

The headline

Contrary to what you might expect, the headline will only ever be read by one person – the editor or journalist you send it to. However much they like it, they will always rewrite it if they use the story. Your press release goes to lots of other journalists, and they don't want to risk duplicating the same headline as another paper. So it will be rewritten as a matter of course. This means that you are not trying to devise a headline that will grab 10 000 readers' attention; you're only trying to grab the 20 or 50-odd people you've sent it to.

105

The journalists whose desk your release lands on are going to throw away four out of five press releases they see. The headline is the fastest way to promote yourself into the top 20%. Imagine a journalist leafing through a pile of press releases, reading only the headlines and occasionally, perhaps, skimming the next few lines. What will make your headline jump out at them? It needs to tell them instantly:

- what the story is
- that it's interesting enough to appeal to their readers.

That's it. The headline needs to do this as quickly and effectively as possible. And that's all it needs to do. The way to achieve this effect on the journalist is to:

- keep it punchy – about five to ten words
- don't try to be clever – just tell them what the story is
- avoid jargon, abbreviations and punctuation
- use active verbs. Don't say 'Roses are bought by more gardeners', say 'More gardeners buy roses'
- be as specific as you can. So change 'More gardeners buy roses' to 'Twice as many gardeners buy roses today than they did in

1985'

- make it sound as interesting as you can: 'New fashion for roses doubles sales in 10 years'.

The first paragraph

If your headline did its job properly, you have now won yourself about another 10 seconds of the journalists' attention. It is almost certainly during this 10 seconds that they will decide whether or not to print your story (or it might go into an 'if there's room' pile). The journalist will almost certainly devote these 10 seconds to reading the first paragraph. That's probably all they'll read, unless after that they decide that they like the story.

If you're a great raconteur or joke-teller, you'll find it really grates to write press releases. Because one of the most important rules of press releases is to give the punchline first. Put the main points that will 'sell' your release to the journalist in this paragraph – the number of jobs you've just created, the name of the celebrity who will open next month's exhibition – whatever is most likely to grab their attention.

Don't bother with the details here – which sites the new jobs will be located in, or what time the opening ceremony is – these can wait till later. In fact, you won't have room to mention it, because this paragraph should also be brief – no more than two sentences at the most, about 35–45 words, and it should make sense on its own. The rest of the press release should simply flesh it out. Include your organisation's name in the first paragraph, if you can, but not if it means sacrificing the clarity of the press release.

The contents

When it comes to writing the rest of the release, there is one important thing you need to know: when journalists and editors cut articles, they always cut them from the bottom up. They haven't time to take out a word here and a sentence there, they just delete the final paragraph, or the final two or three paragraphs. So the more important something is, the nearer the beginning you should put it. If you couldn't get your company name in the first paragraph, put it in the second.

Now you want to explain the basic facts, in clear, plain English (the guidelines for writing plain English are mentioned on page 73). This is not an advertisement, and it should be written as if it were produced by the paper. So refer to your company in the third person, and don't use phrases like 'amazing new product'. You need to answer the questions who, what, when, why, where and how. For example:

- *Who* Gemma Stewart of Felcan Petfoods
- *What* received a cheque for £500 from the Managing Director
- *When* last Friday
- *Why* for coming up with the most profitable staff suggestion of the year
- *Where* the cheque was handed over at a special lunch held in the boardroom
- *How* Gemma earned the award by suggesting a new product line – mouse-flavoured cat food – which looks set to earn the company over £10 000 next year.

After that you can give any background information, and include any quotes you can. Quotes are always a good idea; they add a human dimension. The best way to get quotes out of people – customers, the managing director or whoever – is to invent what you'd like them to say, write it down and then ask them to approve it. Name the people you are quoting (rather than 'a spokesperson for the company said . . .') and quote people who are as relevant, interesting or senior as possible.

The layout

- Head the page 'PRESS RELEASE'.
- Under this, give the release date. This will either read 'For immediate release' or 'Embargoed until . . . (time and date)'. The point of this is that you may want to forewarn the press about your new product launch, but you don't want them print-

Arabesque

PRESS RELEASE

For immediate release

NEW FASHION FOR ROSES DOUBLES SALES IN 10 YEARS

Twice as many people in Britain bought roses last year as did ten years ago, according to a new survey.

Local plant frame company Arabesque took part in the national survey of garden and plant sales companies this year, to find out what the latest trends in rose growing are. Over 500 companies contributed information on this year's sales, which totalled about 25,000 roses across the UK.

Old fashioned roses seem to be the most popular, closely followed by hybrid teas, and climbing roses seem to be gaining in popularity. The survey revealed that pink is still the most popular colour for roses, although 78% of people consider that red is the most romantic colour.

Arabesque's Director, Robin Jones, commented, 'We've certainly noticed that more people seem to be ordering climbing roses to grow against the frames we supply. A lot of the less common old fashioned varieties seem to be making a comeback too, such as moss roses and hybrid musks.'

END

4.11.1994
Contact: Robin Jones, Arabesque, 4 High Street, Alster CD8 9XV
Phone: 0123 456789 (day) or 0987 654321 (evening/weekend)

ing the details before it happens. By and large the press do respect embargoes.

■ Keep your press releases short – try to stick to one side of A4 paper. If you have to go on to use a second page, put 'more' at the bottom of the first page, and start a fresh sheet – don't type on the back of the first page. Identify the second page in case it becomes separated from the first, with your company name, the title of the press release and the page number.

■ Double space the text so there is room for editors to make their own annotations.

■ When you reach the end of the text intended for publication, type 'END'.

■ After the end, put the date.

■ After the date, give a contact name, address, and phone number for further information. It helps to give an evening/ weekend telephone number if you can.

Following up the press release

Don't pester journalists by ringing them every week to ask if they got your latest release. But every so often, if there's one particular publication you specially want to cover a story, and you can offer extra information to them, give them a ring.

Monitoring the results

Companies with money to spare often use press cutting and monitoring agencies, which send them copies of anything that is printed about them. For some large organisations this is useful and cost effective. However, if you can't afford this, you still need to monitor the results of your press releases. This will tell you which stories attract most press interest, and which publications are most helpful to you. To do this:

■ keep all the clippings you can, and put them in a scrap book

■ keep a copy of each release on file, with a note of how many column inches the press collectively gave it. Of course it matters whether its 18 inches of column space was in *The Times* or the *Borchester Echo* but, once the file begins to build up, you'll find that you can get a picture of which kind of stories are most likely to be printed, and in which papers

- some local charities have their own free version of a clippings service – they use volunteers to trawl the local press for references to their organisation, and send them in to the PR officer. Commercial companies with a strong local profile might find staff to do this – find one person who already reads each of the local papers, including freesheets, and ask them simply to clip anything they see on the company.

DEALING WITH THE PRESS AT AN EVENT

If you are holding any kind of event or press conference, invite journalists well ahead of the function. Give them clear details of the time, date and location, as well as the gist of what the event is for. Mid-morning is a good time, and don't expect them to stay longer than about 30–45 minutes. If you hold an event at a time that looks as if it will drag on (such as 12.30 running into lunch) they are less likely to turn up.

Prepare the location, and your own staff. Clean up the building, make sure everyone knows the press will be around, and warn them if they might be photographed. It's a good idea to give the press and your staff name badges.

Make the press welcome – look as if you're expecting them, call them by name (if you can), have someone senior greet them and so on. Offer them a glass of wine or a sandwich, and generally look after them. After all, they're important to you.

Make sure they have all the information they want. Hand out press packs (after the event, so they don't read them during it and miss what's going on), have staff available to talk to them and answer questions, and allow their photographers as much freedom as you can.

PHOTOGRAPHS

Look through any paper. Most of the photographs are mugshots, or people handing each other cheques while grinning fixedly at the camera. You have to compete with these – shouldn't be too difficult, should it? The press are far more likely to print your photographs if they're interesting. If they are eye-catching enough, they may even print a story they would otherwise have excluded.

So the question is, what makes an interesting photograph? It helps if the photograph has action and movement in it, and it is far better to show somebody using your product than holding it, or handing over a cheque with the product not even in the picture. So, for example, if you're announcing that you've just sold 100 yards of Arabesque fencing to the local council to go round their car park, don't have a photograph of you and the Council's Chairperson shaking hands. Persuade one of the senior council officials to come to your site, and photograph them in casual clothes coaxing clematis up one of your frames. Or try an unusual art photograph of them (not looking at the camera) smelling a rose.

It's really worth having a professional photographer take your photos, at least for important stories. But you can manage on a budget if you have a good amateur photographer around – perhaps a member of staff – and you're prepared to guide them and 'direct' the pictures yourself. If you're very strapped for cash, you may find that the local amateur photography club or college students will help out occasionally for the experience.

Photograph everything you can – make it a habit to take a photographer, professional or amateur, to every event, however small. You'll slowly build up a library of photographs of your staff, regular events, sites, products and so on. You'll be surprised how often you use it. Your news stories may need to be up-to-the-minute, but very often a library photograph of the relevant director or product, or last year's annual craft fair, will do fine. They can also be very useful when you're putting together brochures, annual reports and catalogues.

Take everything you can in black and white, as this is what the press will usually want, but take colour photos if you will be sending them to a magazine that usually prints in colour. If you're not sure which is best, ring them and ask. Try to send photographs with your press releases when you can – your article is far more likely to be read. After the headline, people will usually look at the photograph and read the caption if they do nothing else. But if you really can't afford to send them out to everyone, send them to the publications you would most like to print them, and type 'photographs available on request' at the bottom of everyone else's press release.

Remember that photographs should always have full explanatory captions stuck on the back of them. They should be somewhere around 8 × 6 inches, and as sharp as possible – they can lose a lot of contrast in printing, especially on to newsprint. Magazines that print colour photographs will probably want transparencies rather than prints.

RUNNING COMPETITIONS IN THE PAPERS

One more thing before we finish looking at press PR. It can be surprisingly easy to persuade the press to run a competition offering your product or service as a prize. The idea, of course, is that everyone who loses was so looking forward to having one of your holidays, swimming pools, diaries or whatever you produce, that they come and buy one from you. The press like it because it helps to attract and keep readers – competitions are always very popular.

You could run an Arabesque competition in one of the gardening magazines or a Sunday colour supplement, or perhaps even the local paper. And you'd organise it for March or April, when people are busy thinking about their gardens. You could offer an Arabesque free-standing frame to the winner and a £15-off voucher on Arabesque products to the first ten runners up – then they'll have to come and buy something from you to get any benefit. Obviously the more you are prepared to offer, the more enthusiastic the newspaper or magazine will be.

You will, of course, want the names and addresses of everyone who enters the competition so that you can contact them subsequently, so talk to the newspaper or magazine about the arrangements for this.

Business to business competitions, for example in trade

magazines, can be difficult to get a good response to. Why should someone care if they win five free reams of photocopier paper? It's no skin off their nose to order it on the business account and let the company pay for it.

If you're going to offer something to businesses, offer something that will appeal to the person filling out the form and that they wouldn't be able to buy on the company account. Some kind of business luxury, for example, that the company wouldn't want to pay for, but the customers themselves would want on a personal level. For instance, first class travel for a month on your commuter coach service, or a luxury set of desk accessories.

Getting on the radio

The guidelines for getting on the radio are similar to those for getting into the papers (except that you can forget the photographs). You should send all your local press releases to your local radio stations as well. As with the press, you need to think like a customer in order to devise the most promising stories. Again, as with the local press, could you present a monthly five-minute gardening spot, or comment on stories about fire safety or tourism or whatever your industry is?

QUESTIONS TO ASK BEFORE YOU SAY 'YES' TO DOING AN INTERVIEW

There are certain ways in which you can be caught out, or at least caught unawares, when you give radio interviews – especially live ones. Here's a checklist of questions to ensure that nothing takes you by surprise.

- *Will it be live or recorded?* Live interviews are more nerve-wracking than recorded ones because if you say the wrong thing, it will be broadcast. On the other hand, you can be misrepresented in a taped interview, as the editor could select comments out of context to broadcast that sound different to how you intended.

- *What will the line of questioning be?* The interviewer is unlikely to tell you in advance what questions they will ask you, but they may give you an idea of the subject areas. If you are there as the local expert on fire safety, you want to be sure that the questions will be within your range of expertise, or you could come out looking foolish.

- *How long will it last?* You often only get 30 seconds to 4 minutes on the radio, but do ask; occasionally a reporter may decide to interview you for 30 minutes. If you've assumed you'll be lucky to get three minutes, you could be stuck for anything useful to say if this happens.

- *Will there be other people with you?* Find out who – if you're defending a decision to close down a factory, you don't want to find out five minutes before you go on air that an irate union spokesperson will also be on the programme.

- *Will there be a phone-in?* You will need to be prepared for anything if there is. On the other hand, you can always ask friends and colleagues to call with questions that you can answer so as to put your company in a good light.

114

You'll have to decide whether or not you want to do the interview. The answer is often that it's better not to. Just one additional point to consider though. If you decide not to be interviewed about a controversial topic that may show your organisation in a bad light, the reporter is likely to say, 'We invited someone from XYZ Ltd to put their point of view, but they declined to come on the show', which tends to give the impression that you have something to hide, even though this may not be the case at all. Don't forget to take this into account when balancing up the pros and cons of doing the interview.

HOW TO PREPARE FOR A RADIO INTERVIEW

You don't want to come away from a radio interview feeling that you didn't manage to get your point across, or worse still that you made a complete mess of answering an unexpected question. So think ahead, and prepare yourself before you ever get near the microphone:

■ decide what you want to say and say it no matter what they ask you. You may only get a few seconds, so condense your main points right down or you may not have time to put them across. If you want an example of how to say what *you* want to instead of answering the question, you can pick up plenty of tips by watching any politician on television – they say things like, 'That's an interesting question, but before I answer it, I'd just like to say . . .'

■ work out what the interviewer is likely to ask and have an answer ready. The interviewer's job is to represent the listener. So think, if you were the listener, what would you want to know? Prepare yourself for the worst possible questions – they probably won't be asked, but you'll be ready if they are.

■ ask a colleague or a friend to 'interview' you as a rehearsal, and encourage them to be as challenging and as difficult as they like.

115

Don't be surprised if the radio station interviews you by phone, at home or in your office. Treat this like a normal interview, but make sure that you are somewhere quiet, and if there are other people around, post someone at the door to keep them quiet.

HANDLING THE INTERVIEW

■ If you're being interviewed at the radio station, make sure you arrive early. If you travel by car, listen to the radio station on the way, and find out if they're trailing your spot, what their angle on the subject is, and what they're saying about you.

■ Resist the temptation to have a drink 'to help you relax' before the interview.

■ If you need to go to the loo just before the interview starts, say so. Most people need to.

■ Ignore all the technical stuff. The technicians will make sure that you can be heard properly, and that your microphone is in the right place. Just concentrate on the conversation.

- Forget about all the listeners, just concentrate on the interviewer you're talking to.

- Don't gabble. This is particularly hard when you're expecting them to cut you off at any moment, but it's not worth it – the listeners will miss everything you say if you rush it.

- The listeners have no picture, only sound to entertain them, so don't allow your voice to degenerate to a monotone or they won't listen.

- Remember that you can hear a smile, even on the radio.

- People will judge you very fast on radio (or television). If you sound at all rude, arrogant, pompous or uncaring, *you* may know that it's totally out of character, but they won't. So try hard to come across as pleasant, friendly and caring.

- Correct any factual inaccuracies straight away. If the interviewer calls you or your company by the wrong name, or says you're taking on 50 new people when it's actually 70, interrupt them (politely) and put them straight, or correct them before you answer the next question.

- If the topic is at all controversial, bear in mind that it is vital to stay cool. You are guaranteed to come across badly if you become irritable or angry. People will take against you, even if you're in the right; it may not be fair, but it's a fact.

Getting on TV

Again, like the other media, you need to send regular press releases to your local television stations. Get to know the journalists if you can, and offer your services as a local expert on whatever it is you do. Be warned that if they do want to use you, or cover your story, you'll be lucky to get 12 hours' notice.

Most of the guidelines for dealing with television interviews are the same as those for radio interviews: you'll need to ask the same questions, and prepare your answers in the same way. There are one or two extra points on handling the interview itself, though:

- don't try to watch the cameras, you'll distract yourself and you'll distract the viewers
- try not to think about your mannerisms or gestures, and they should look fine (though if you know you have a particular frequent mannerism try to tone it down)
- if you're in a studio, don't assume the interview has finished until the studio manager tells you so
- if you're being filmed at your offices or factory, make sure you're happy with what's in the background of the shot – don't let the cameras film the dirtiest corner of the delivery yard.

WHAT TO WEAR

In order to decide what to wear, you'll have to decide on the image you want to project. A uniform will make you look formal and authoritarian, for example; a white coat will look scientific or professional; casual clothes will look friendly and informal. If you are being presented in a way that you don't like, dress to give the opposite impression. If your company is being accused of a dictatorial approach to its staff, wear something friendly and casual (without going to extremes, of course); if you are being criticised for lax safety precautions, wear something smart and professional.

Once you have settled the question of your image, you can think about the specific clothes:

- wear something you're already comfortable in – don't buy a new outfit for the occasion
- you'll be hot, especially if you're in a studio, so wear fabrics that are cool and don't show sweat
- large expanses of black or white are not good for technical reasons (to do with flare and contrast)
- steer clear of narrow stripes and checks – they can turn positively psychedelic on the screen
- don't wear anything that is so showy it detracts from your face (ties, earrings and so on) or people will be distracted and stop listening to what you're saying

117

- sunglasses are not the best thing to wear as they tend to make you look suspicious; they also reduce the viewer's ability to focus on what you're saying, because they can't see your eyes
- ordinary, clear glasses are fine. And don't worry – the technicians will make sure they don't reflect.

Crisis management

Crises can cost a fortune in damages, lost working time, extra work, and lost sales as a result of damaging publicity. As we can't afford to lose this kind of money, we need to make sure that if we do hit a crisis we can limit the damage as far as possible. Some crises are unpredictable, such as:

- structural damage as a result of fire, flood or other natural disasters
- serious injury or fatality at your factory or site
- food poisoning scare in the canteen.

However, other crises you can anticipate reasonably far ahead:

- staff going on strike
- redundancies
- poor annual results
- product recalls.

These lists are clearly far from comprehensive, and there will be some potential disasters specific to you. At Arabesque, for example, a major clematis blight could be a serious problem. Some disasters will receive sympathetic coverage from the press, while others could invite damaging publicity.

The important thing to remember about all media relations, and crises in particular, is that the truth doesn't count – the only thing that matters is what people *perceive* to be the truth. If you leap over-enthusiastically to your own defence, without evidence to back up your case, no matter how valid your position is people will be inclined to think, 'Well, they would say that, wouldn't they?'

Expect a negative response and at worst you'll be prepared – and at best you'll be pleasantly surprised.

PREPARING FOR A CRISIS

The first thing to do, before you hit trouble, is to form a permanent Crisis Team. This team will take over in the event of a crisis. There are plenty of things you can do in advance, without knowing what the crisis is:

- appoint a spokesperson who will talk to the media in the event of a crisis – this could always be the same person, or it could vary according to the nature of the crisis. Either way, it must be a member of the team
- write the press releases for any reasonably likely disasters in advance and keep them on file. In an emergency, the last thing you'll feel like doing is writing a press release – this way you'll only have to fill in the gaps
- prepare any other letters (which the press may well see in the event), such as letters to customers recalling faulty products and so on
- keep emergency press packs, with copies of safety records, details of evacuation procedures, and so on
- keep up-to-date safety and security information on file
- plan how you would cope with an influx of media people. Where would you put a press room? How would switchboard cope?
- train the spokesperson or people in how to deal with the media.

HANDLING THE CRISIS

If you volunteer the information the media want, there's a chance they'll go away happy and look no further. If you withhold it, they may go and talk to disgruntled ex-employees, union officials or local campaigners to find out what they want. So you should always tell them anything you can.

The big mistake most companies make with the media is to take the wrong attitude. We hit maybe one big crisis every couple of years at most; they deal with them all the time. They know a hundred times more about how to get the best story than we will ever know about how to hide it. And the story we *really* can't afford to risk is that we've been caught trying to cover something up. Look at the unpopularity that the drug companies generate when they continue to sell drugs after danger warnings from scientists. So we have to co-operate with the press whether we like it or not. In fact, what we want is to get them on our side. There's a handful of important groundrules for dealing with the media during a crisis.

- *be honest* remember Richard Nixon? Not only does lying rarely work, but if you are ever found out everyone will believe you were lying about everything all the time

- *keep in contact with the media* the more information you hand them, the less they will need to dig around in the dirt to find a good story

- *treat the media with respect* remember that they're only doing their job. You may not like it, but if there are hordes of them around your door it's because this is a good story. You want them on your side, so treat them well – let them use the phone if they need to, or offer them coffee if they're outside for hours in the cold. What have you got to lose?

- *be friendly and positive* if you come across as worried or negative in interviews, people will assume you're in trouble. If you appear angry (however legitimately) they'll take agin you. So always be courteous and positive, but don't be over cheerful if the crisis has caused people to suffer – casualities, redundancies and so on

- *retain a human face* the press know that people are at the heart of any good story. That's why when 500 people are made redundant, they'll interview the employees to ask how they're going to cope; and when there's a fire, they'll talk to relatives of the casualties. These pictures will go next to your interview when they run the story. So don't forget to show sympathy and a caring attitude towards anyone who has suffered as a result of the problem – even if you don't accept responsibility

- *go further than you need to put things right* what you really want is for the press to run a story saying what a wonderful company you are. So give them the opportunity. If an employee is injured when working abroad, fly their immediate family out to visit them. Or recall all possible products at the first whiff of a problem – the drug manufacturers Johnson & Johnson did this when three people in Chicago fell ill after taking Tylenol capsules that had been laced with cyanide. They recalled every bottle of Tylenol in the US, and designed new, tamper-proof packaging within six weeks. It turned out that the problem was, in fact, limited to the Chicago area, and the culprit was caught; Johnson & Johnson weren't to blame. But the speed and extent of their response earned them huge credibility – six months later they came fifth in a national survey of most admired companies

- and finally, the one rule worth writing in ten-foot high letters on the wall of the crisis team's office: **Never say: 'No comment'**. Every time we hear anyone say 'No comment' in a radio, TV or press story what do we instantly assume? That they're guilty, of course. They may not be guilty, but we'll all think it anyway. But people tend to forget this when it's their turn; especially if *they* know they're innocent. Unfortunately, however, it doesn't matter what *you* know to be the truth. Just remember that every time you say 'No comment', it will translate in every listener's mind as 'I'm guilty as hell.'

121

COPING WITH DIFFICULT INTERVIEWS

It's worth being prepared for some of the techniques that interviewers use to put you under pressure. So here are a few of the more common ones, and how to respond to them.

Question	Response
The hypothetical 'What if . . .' question.	'I can't discuss a hypothetical question. Let's talk about the facts.'
They say 'Industry sources claim . . .'.	'I can't answer a blind accusation. You'll have to be more specific about the source.' Don't repeat the allegation.

They fire machine gun questions at you.	Stay calm and ask, 'Which question would you like me to answer first?'
They keep interrupting you.	Wait for them to finish the new question, say, 'I'll answer that in a moment', and then continue what you were saying before.
They say nothing.	They are trying to psych you into filling the silence, by putting your foot in it. Say nothing. If anyone looks foolish it will be them – the onus is on them to keep the interview flowing.
They summarise what you've said, wrongly.	Keep cool, and reiterate what you actually said.

Non-media PR

There are plenty of other forms of PR – in fact the range is as broad as your imagination. Anything that is interesting enough to draw people's attention to your business in a positive way is PR. Here, briefly, are a few of the more common forms of non-media PR.

TALKS

Lots of organisations arrange talks. Could you offer to speak to your local school, WI or gardening club?

SPONSORSHIP

This can be very cost effective, but only if you *target* it. Go back to rule one, *think*. Where is the most effective place to put your money? Could you give the prize money for the best rose at the county agricultural show? Or sponsor something that potential customers will remember because your name has a link with it? For example, one large manufacturer of matches sponsored a regional theatre company's production of *The Matchmaker*. It was worth it because it was memorable.

LOCAL DONATIONS

You're bound to be asked to make donations to all sorts of worthy local causes. It's a bad idea not to co-operate, because it will get you a bad name ('they *never* give anything . . .'), and even if your customers aren't local, at least some of your staff presumably are, so you need to preserve a friendly image. If you are on a small budget you have two options, really. Either you can donate in kind, if you have access to any useful products (possibly rejects or second-hand), or you can set aside a sum, however small, for local donations. Divide this equally between all the local causes that ask, and let them know that they're all getting about the same.

OPEN DAYS

Invite customers and potential customers to spend half a day looking around your site. This needn't be expensive, just provide a few sandwiches and wine or even just orange juice for lunch. You may want to separate some categories of customer, such as public and business customers, and hold one open day for each. Or invite visits and attachments from local school and college students.

123

EVENTS AND PARTIES

The guidelines are similar to those for open days, but build the event around something special, such as five years in business or a new product launch. Sometimes you'll invite your customers to the same event as the media, but there are times when you want to invite the media separately so you can give them more attention.

FREE GIFTS

Christmas cards, a free tank of petrol when you buy a new car, flowers in the hotel room when the customer arrives, a guide on how to choose and care for climbing plants that comes free with every Arabesque climbing frame – these are all a part of PR. The point is that you're doing something extra for your customers to make them feel special. That way, they're more likely to come back again. Do make sure that you cost these carefully though – too many companies provide extras like this and then discover too late that it is an unaffordable expense – and it's difficult to stop doing it once you've started.

NEWSLETTERS

These don't have to be expensive, and they can be a far better targeted (and therefore cost effective) way of publicising your products or services, and your company in general, than advertising. You can keep your costs down by producing as few as three a year (less than this gives your customers time to forget you between issues), and it can be just two sides of A4. The guidelines in Chapter 4 should give you plenty of design ideas for putting a newsletter together in-house or printing it cheaply.

124

A good newsletter should contain news stories (such as new products or services) and features that show the company in a good light (such as how one of your customers increased productivity by using your product), but *don't* try to hard sell in a newsletter – it damages your credibility. Other sections you could include are:

- ideas for new ways to use the product/service
- question and answer section
- events calendar
- statistics about your industry (people tend to find statistics interesting)
- 'how to . . .' guides to using your products, directly or indirectly, for example 'How to add on sections of Arabesque fencing' or 'How to treat clematis wilt'.

PR is really all about thinking from the point of view of the reader, listener, viewer or recipient. And it is central to low cost marketing because, if you use it wisely, you can get an enormous return for almost no outlay.

6

Advertising

Half the money I spend on advertising is wasted. The trouble is I never know which half.

Lord Leverhulme

A lot of businesses seem happier to throw money away on advertising than on anything else. The reason seems to be that they ignore rule one — *think*. They assume that as long as they put an advertisement in the paper they will increase their business. For a few companies this may be true, but for most it simply doesn't work like that.

125

But these companies with cash to throw around often never find out that they're making a mistake. Why not? For two reasons: first, they don't know what constitutes success or failure in their advertising, and second, they can't tell how much business the advertisement generated.

As we can't afford to make these kinds of mistakes, we'll have to think before we advertise. And we can structure that thinking by asking the following five questions.

1 Who are we talking to?
2 Where are they?
3 What do we hope to gain?
4 What do we want to say?
5 How will we know if it has worked?

Let's look at each of these in turn.

Who are we talking to?

This question may not take long to answer, but you must ask it. After all, if *you* don't know who they are, how will they know? Draw up a profile of the people you want to communicate with. Are they:

- local, regional, national, international
- customers, potential customers, ex-customers, new customers
- business people, professionals, specialists, general public, retailers, agencies?

Once you have decided who you want to talk to in terms of their relationship with you, define them even more precisely by looking at what type of people they are:

- probable age range
- male/female ratio
- income level
- interests
- type of business
- probable job title.

And so on. You should know this information already, through a combination of research and common sense. Be careful not to make wrong assumptions. For example, if you sell mountaineering safety equipment, don't assume that most of your customers will be young, fit mountaineers. They might be, but do your research and make sure. There could be a lot of parents who buy expensive pieces of safety equipment as presents for their enthusiast children.

The more accurate your profile is, the less money you need to waste. You may have two or three different groups of people you want to communicate with. That's fine. Identify them all separately because you may need to reach them all in different ways. For example, you may want to advertise your safety equipment to budding mountaineers and their relatives, but you would probably want to say something different to each group. For example, you'll want to tell the mountaineers how professional they'll look, as well as how safe they'll be. You'll probably want to tell the relatives that if they give this equipment to their loved ones, they won't have to lie awake at night worrying about them any more.

Where are they?

This is possibly the most vital question for people without money to spare. You don't want to pay a fortune for an advertisement that reaches three million homes, if only a hundred of those readers fit your target profile. This is the reason so many people throw money away when they advertise. If you only have 50 potential customers, don't advertise on national television. You need to target very specifically if you're on a low budget – use bullets not buckshot.

THINK LIKE A CUSTOMER

What sort of products or services do you buy from advertisements in the local paper, for instance? Second-hand cars, puppies and kittens, houses, logs (if you live in a rural area) – that sort of thing. You say to yourself, 'I wonder if there are any second-hand fridge-freezers advertised in the paper this week', and you scan the advertising section. Anyone wanting to sell a fridge-freezer could do far worse than advertise it in the local paper.

However, most local papers are full of advertisements which you'd never be looking for. To give you a few genuine examples (all taken from a single issue of a local paper): a sports injuries clinic, a vegetarian nursing home and a knacker's yard. What proportion of the paper's readers do you suppose are suffering from a sports injury on any given date?

To advertise cost effectively, you need to think like a customer. The key question to ask yourself about your own product or service is: 'If I wanted to buy this, where would I look to find someone who was selling it?'

EXAMINE ALL THE OPTIONS

You often find that you wouldn't look in a newspaper at all. You'd look in the *Yellow Pages* (say, for an emergency plumber), or in a specialist magazine, or you'd call a trade association and ask them for a list of local suppliers. Maybe your potential customers don't know that your product or service exists; where could you advertise it so that it would catch their eye? There are thousands of ways to advertise, so think about which makes the most sense for your customers.

Places to advertise

Newspapers and magazines
These include:

- local papers
- national papers
- freesheets
- trade and professional publications
- general interest magazines
- specialist magazines
- subscription magazines
- in-house magazines
- parish magazines
- foreign newspapers and magazines.

There are two basic types of newspaper and magazine advertisement: *classified* and *display*. Classifieds are the short advertisements that only consist of a line or two each and are usually 'classified' under headings, hence the name. This is where you sell your second-hand washing machine in the local paper or your pedigree kittens in the specialist cat magazines.

Display advertisements have to be designed (however simply), and are sold in column inches (for example, 2 columns wide by 3 inches high is a total of 6 column inches) or in full pages, half pages, quarters, eighths and so on.

Any newspaper or magazine should be able to tell you its circulation and its readership. These are not the same thing: the circulation tells you how many copies are circulated, but each copy might be read by several people. Think of all the copies of *Country*

Life and *Reader's Digest* you see in doctors' waiting rooms. One copy could be read by dozens of people, and, of course, you'll need to know what kind of people read them. If you advertise valuable antiques in *Country Life*, you can't assume that every reader is a potential customer. However, you will need to find out how many of the readers do fit your target profile, in order to decide how cost-effective the advertisement is. A cheap advertisement in your local freesheet that only reaches three potential customers may not be nearly as cost effective as an expensive advertisement in a trade magazine that lands on the desks of 300 prospects.

Bear in mind as well that the more people pay for a publication, the more likely they are to read it. The local freesheet may go to every house in your area, but how many people will just put it straight in the bin without reading it? Subscription magazines usually get a very good response. Readers are not only paying for them, but committing themselves to paying for them for a whole year, so they're obviously interested in reading them. In fact, 60% of magazine subscribers read more than half the advertisements in them.

Broadcast media
These include:

- regional or national television
- local radio
- foreign radio or television
- local cinema.

This kind of advertising is sold in time slots – usually 10 to 60 seconds. The cost of this will vary according to the time of day you want the advertisement broadcast. This is often high cost advertising because you will have to find a professional to put the advertisement together for you, quite apart from paying for the airtime. But if it reaches your audience effectively, it may be cost effective.

If you do want to use this medium, try to find a freelance or small production company to make the advertisement – they'll be cheaper because their overheads will be lower. Be very thorough

129

about asking for references, seeing examples of previous work and shopping around for quotes.

This is a classic time to follow rule four of low cost marketing: *keep it simple*. Even with professionals doing the work, it's worth remembering that the more 'flashy' you try to be, the bigger the potential disaster you are inviting. A good producer should be capable of coming up with an effective advertisement for you without having to use gimmicks, special effects or expensive actors.

You can look up the agencies who sell this form of advertising in *BRAD* (British Rate and Data), which should be available in your nearest main library.

Posters and signs

These include:

- hoardings
- railway and coach stations
- buses and trains
- your vehicles
- signs outside your shop, warehouse, pick-your-own fruit farm or whatever.

The agencies that sell billboard and transport advertising are listed in *BRAD*, along with the broadcast media agencies. As far as your vehicle or shop is concerned, don't waste space. If you can put a sign outside your shop or on your vehicles, do it, for goodness' sake (if you haven't already). However, remember that people will judge you by your signs. If you have an expensive shop that sells luxury goods, don't put a tatty old sign in the street – it sends out the wrong message.

When it comes to painting signs on your cars, vans or lorries, the same thing applies. If you don't keep the vehicles clean, it gives a bad impression. Also, watch that the drivers are courteous – I have to confess that there is one company whose products I never buy because one of their vans cut me up really badly on a roundabout a few years ago. People will judge your business by the chivalry of your drivers and how clean your vans are, as much as by anything you actually write on the sign.

Directories

These include:

- *Yellow Pages*
- trade directories (contact the trade association or publishers)
- yearbooks.

Any 24-hour plumber who doesn't advertise in *Yellow Pages* deserves to go out of business. On the other hand, if you're a nuclear power plant, there's not a lot of point. The question is, 'If my customers wanted to buy my product/service, where would they look for someone who was selling it?' If you think your customers are likely to look you up in *Yellow Pages*, take out a display advertisement. And think carefully about which category your customers would look you up under – you may need to have two or three entries; perhaps Arabesque should be under both Garden supplies and Fencing.

Contact the publisher of trade directories and yearbooks, or the trade association that produces them, for details of their advertising charges.

Brochures and leaflets

These include:

- handbills
- leaflets through letterboxes
- point-of-sale material
- leaflets in related businesses (such as the local gym if you run a sports injury clinic).

A lot of local newspapers and local youth groups will distribute leaflets through letterboxes. This is relatively inexpensive, and can be useful for domestic addresses. If they are distributing on trading estates, however, the leaflet will probably never make it past the receptionist. So unless you are selling a product for receptionists, it may not pay to do this. It could be better to mail direct (see Chapter 7).

It can be quite easy to persuade a local business that shares customers with you to display your leaflets. Rather than offering to pay them for doing so, why not offer to display their leaflets in your premises in exchange?

Other places
These include:

- car park tickets, bus tickets and so on
- calendars and wall planners
- pens to give away
- T-shirts
- books of matches.

Car park and bus tickets often say on them, 'To advertise in this space, call ...'. Lots of businesses will print your name on calendars, pens, T-shirts and a host of other items at varying costs. Look them up in *Yellow Pages* under Promotional items (a perfect example of a business that should be in *Yellow Pages*).

TARGET AS TIGHTLY AS POSSIBLE

That may seem like a long list but it's not comprehensive – I haven't even mentioned hot air balloons and sky signs – because the options are as broad as your imagination. The important thing is to define your audience as precisely as possible, and then select the medium that targets this audience as precisely as possible. It may not be what you originally had in mind at all.

One producer of malt whisky in Scotland wanted to advertise his malt whisky, which he sold nationally through retailers, mostly pubs and off licences. He was lucky enough to have a few thousand to spend, so he approached an advertising agency. After talking to him and asking him questions, the agency told him his few thousand pounds was either too little (for a national campaign) or too much (for a targeted approach). They came up with a quite different suggestion.

They established that he only really needed to sell his whisky to the retailers, as they could sell it to the public far more effectively than he could. This meant that he only really had about a dozen or so main customers: the big breweries which owned the pubs, and the major off licence chains. So they suggested that he forget about national magazine advertising, and hold a special event for the chief buyers of these few vital outlets instead.

He invited them all on a paid trip to Scotland for the day to visit his distillery and sample his whisky. It cost about half what he would have spent on advertising, and he got to speak directly to all his most important prospects. It just shows what common sense thinking can do – the only difference for us is that we can't afford to pay an agency to do our thinking for us, we have to do it for ourselves.

Resist temptation

Advertising should be proactive, not reactive. In other words, you need to plan and allocate your budget. Target your advertising as accurately as you can. This means that if you decide local news-paper advertising is not the best use of your precious money, don't do it – even when the local paper rings you to try to sell you advertising space, as they almost undoubtedly will.

A very useful rule here, especially if you know you are prone to be impulsive, is never to make a buying decision in the presence of the salesperson, and don't allow them to put pressure on you either. The press are inclined to invite you to place a 'support ad'. This is when they run a feature on a local business or charity, and encourage that business' suppliers to advertise in support. The implication is that the featured business (which you supply) won't be happy if you don't advertise.

If a charity is featured, the salesperson may even suggest that you don't care about sick children, the ozone layer or whatever the charity is concerned with. Don't rise to this. Just say that you have a company policy never to buy advertising over the phone, and ask them to send you their media pack (an information pack that includes their rate card, or price list).

I don't want to imply that all advertising salespeople are unethical emotional blackmailers – they certainly aren't – but it's worth knowing how to handle the pushy ones; failure to do so has been the cause of many a misguided advertisement. If newspaper advertisements are not on your well thought out advertising plan, don't change your mind just because there's a good salesperson at the other end of the phone. If they tell you that this space will only cost you £40 instead of the usual £60, you will not be saving £20, whatever they tell you. You will be throwing away £40.

What do we hope to gain?

Presumably, you want to increase business. However, when the newspaper, directory, bus company or whoever you advertised with comes back to try to sell you another advertisement, how will you know whether the last one worked? What was it trying to achieve: a 100% increase in sales? Two telephone enquiries? The only way you'll know is if you set objectives for every advertisement you place; then you'll be able to check later whether it met its objective or not. The sort of objectives you might have are to:

- raise awareness of your product or service
- generate leads
- generate sales
- inform customers that you are moving, attending a particular exhibition or whatever
- recruit staff, agents and so on.

COSTING YOUR ADVERTISEMENTS

In each case, you need to be as specific as you can – how many enquiries? sales worth how much? how many job applications, of what standard? It's all very well saying be specific, but how are you supposed to know what targets to set?

It all comes down to money – it's just a simple balancing act really. Work out what the advertisement will cost you, not forgetting to include your time. That's the end of the calculation, really. The advertisement must generate more profit than this figure to be worth doing.

Of course, it's not quite that simple. You can't be certain to the nearest few pence exactly how much income the advertisement will generate. So unless it's a regular advertisement that you have learned to predict very accurately, you'd better aim to generate a reasonable margin more than your costs. The important thing is that your advertisements, of whatever kind, should be earning their keep.

Some objectives are harder to quantify in terms of money than others, but you need to find a way. Raising awareness, or informing customers you've moved, are only worth doing because you hope they will eventually lead to sales – which you reckon you wouldn't get without the advertisement. So work out how many sales you think they will eventually generate. When it comes to recruitment advertising, calculate the value of finding the right person for the job.

135

Shop around

Sometimes you find that you can make your advertisement pay in any one of several positions. In this case, shop around. If we want to advertise Arabesque in a national magazine, we might find that the prices vary enormously between magazines with a similarly targeted readership. Equally, advertising on local buses might be far cheaper than advertising in the local cinema, but could have similar results.

What do we want to say?

The things you say in an advertisement broadly fall into two categories – general and specific. General things are messages about corporate image (quality, good value, down-to-earth products and so on). You can't avoid general messages – even your choice of where and how to advertise will say things about you whether you like it or not. Specifics are messages like 'Visit our showroom now' and 'Buy before the end of November and get one free'.

GENERAL MESSAGES

This is really a question of corporate image, which we looked at in the last chapter. But in the context of advertising, there are a couple of points to make:

- remember that your corporate image should be consistent across the board, and that includes advertising. Your logo, house colours, style and so on should be consistent with all your other printed material. So should the overall impression that you have chosen to project as your corporate image – luxury, cheap prices, traditional style or whatever it is

- look at what your competitors do. If they all take full page colour advertisements in the trade press, you probably ought to do the same, or else advertise in a completely different medium. If you're the only one who takes black and white quarter page advertisements it will look as if you're smaller, tattier or less successful. If you do advertise in the same publication, find a way to capitalise on the style of your advertisements, for example you could say, 'We're a small business, so we can't afford to make mistakes.'

WRITING YOUR OWN ADVERTISEMENTS

Now we come to the nitty-gritty of sitting down and writing the 'specific' part of the advertisement. The principles are the same whether it's going on a bus ticket, a handbill or the back cover of a glossy trade magazine.

There is a standard formula that all good advertisements follow, known as AIDA, which stands for Attention, Interest, Desire, Action.

- *attention* the first thing to do is to grab the reader's attention. You can do this with an illustration, a photograph (people are more likely to 'believe' photographs than drawings) or, most commonly, a headline, for instance, 'How many mountains can you eat?'

- *interest* now that you have the reader's attention, you need to hold their interest: 'Mountain munch is the most filling low-calorie chocolate bar you'll find'
- *desire* the next step is to create a desire for your product or service: 'Crunchy popcorn and chewy toffee enticingly coated in real milk chocolate . . . and only 23 calories a bar'
- *action* and finally, encourage them to take action: 'Go out and buy one now'

Let's examine each of these elements to see how they work.

Attention

Most people scan advertisements in the same way:

- any illustration
- the headline
- the bottom right hand corner, to find out who is advertising.

137

It takes about one and a half seconds for the eye to get this far. If you haven't caught the reader's interest by this stage, they will give up. If they carry on reading, they will move on to:

- the caption under the main illustration (if there is one)
- any subheadings, smaller illustrations or bold type (as long as there's not too much of it)
- the first line of the main text.

Pick up a newspaper or magazine and flick through it. Which advertisements catch your eye? Have a look at them and work out why they grab your attention. Are they particularly large? Or in colour? Or do they have interesting headlines, or unusual pictures? You can learn a lot just by thinking about other people's advertisements.

You know all the advertisements in the local paper for carpet showrooms and plumbers? They're aimed at you. Did they work? What persuaded you, or put you off? A lot of advertisers make the mistake of printing their name larger than anything else, but the customer wants to know about the product, not the manufacturer. They may have lost your attention before you even found out what the product was. Communication with your potential customers doesn't start until they read the advertisement.

The headline is usually the most important part of the advertisement. It will be read by five times as many people as the rest of the advertisement. And there is one thing it must contain above all else: promise. Dr Johnson said, 'The soul of an advertisement is promise – large promise.' What this means is that your readers do not want to know what the product *is*, they want to know what it can *do* for them.

Sell benefits, not features

You need to sell the benefits of your product, not its features. To give you an example, one of the features of Arabesque is that it is plastic coated. The benefit of this is that it is better camouflaged. Another feature is that it is made of aluminium – the benefit of this is that it is light and easy to carry around. If your headline promises a benefit ('You'll feel ten years younger' or 'No more queuing at supermarkets'), it is four times more likely to be read than one that doesn't do so.

The USP

People don't usually concentrate very hard on advertisements – particularly those on buses and hoardings and in newspapers. Probably only around 5% of the readers will read yours. They are more likely to notice your advertisement in a magazine that they've paid for. But even so, you have to do all the work of communicating with them; you can't expect them to meet you half way. Just because you've put a lot of time and expense into the advertisement, they're not going to feel they owe it to you to read it. If you want them to take notice, you need to be very clear and simple. You'll be lucky to get their attention for as long as two seconds, so you only have time to say one thing.

Which one thing? Unless this is a recruitment advertisement or one announcing a special event of some kind, the one thing should be what is known as your Unique Selling Proposition. The one thing that makes your product special – unique. Maybe you

138

deliver faster than anyone else. Maybe you're the only company in your line of business to offer a month's free trial. Maybe your product comes in a wider choice of colours than your competitors'. Perhaps it's the cheapest. Whatever it is, there must be something you can pick out as your USP.

Actually, it doesn't have to be unique, so long as no-one else has mentioned it. For example, a minicab company could say, 'If we can't get to you within 15 minutes, we'll tell you so.' In fact, there may be several cab companies that will tell you so, but none of them has thought to advertise the fact. And once you've said it, you've taken the wind out of their sails.

One of the best examples of a USP I've ever come across is Death cigarettes. They capitalise on the fact that they are the only cigarette company to tell the truth (the cigarette packets say: 'Smoking does not make you sexy, stylish or sophisticated. It kills you'). They use slogans like, 'We're selling a pack of cigarettes, not a pack of lies', and cover their cigarette packets with health warnings. They consolidate this unique image by making it their policy not to target teenagers with their advertising, and giving a large chunk of their profits to non-vivisection cancer research.

Words to use and not to use

Certain words are more likely than others to attract readers. For example, here are some key words that will help you grab their attention:

new	*save*	*guaranteed*	*alternative*
free	*discover*	*bargain*	*love*
you	*results*	*sale*	*comfortable*
introducing	*money off*	*proven*	*healthy*
announcing	*easy*	*now*	*benefits*

By the same token, some words are a turn-off. You might occasionally see them used successfully by professional agencies, but if you or I tried to use them, we'd probably do more harm than good. So play safe, and avoid the following words:

difficult	*worry*	*risk*	*order*
wrong	*fail*	*buy*	*bad*

| *decision* | *contract* | *tax* | *death* |
| *obligation* | *loss* | *cost* | |

Headline dos and don'ts

Over the years, research has turned up all kinds of tips for writing headlines, which you might as well have the benefit of:

- people are more likely to read headlines if they have more than ten words
- be as specific as you can ('9 out of 10 owners . . .', not 'most owners . . .')
- putting the price in the headline makes the advertisement more memorable (but being remembered is not the aim, the aim is to sell. If the price is a good selling point, include it, but don't put it in if it could deter potential customers)
- the following make your headlines harder to read, so people are less likely to make the effort to do so:

  - capital letters
  - italics
  - fancy typefaces (not always, but be sure yours really is easily legible)
  - reversed out type (that's a light type on a dark background, usually white on black).

Remember that these rules apply to leaflets, signs, poster advertising and so on. Here are two genuine examples. A painting and decorating partnership calling themselves, let's say, Smith & Jones, complained that they had stuck business cards on the windscreens of about 500 cars in their area and not had one response. It turned out that their business card looked like this:

Smith & Jones

Painters and Decorators

Phone 0123-456789

There's no promise there; no benefit, no USP. They could only possibly hope to attract the minute proportion of people who had just decided to have their house decorated, but hadn't yet decided who to go to. Had they included a promise, they might have persuaded people who weren't thinking of decorating to consider it.

Take a look at this:

Do you want decorators
who treat your house like a home
and not a building site?

Call Smith & Jones
0123-456789

That's more like it! The second example is of another painting and decorating duo, but this pair understands the value of an attention grabbing line (and of not wasting the space on the side of your van). The sign painted on their vehicle reads:

Patel & Son
Builders and Decorators

You've tried the cowboys
... now try the Indians

Phone: 081-123 4567

Interest

So your headline has hooked them. Now what are you going to say to them? One of the vital things is to focus on the reader. Don't start telling them what your product is called or what it does. Let them see that you understand *them*, and their needs. A lot of businesses are tempted to boast about their product, the awards it has won and so on. An understandable temptation, but one to resist. Yes, the awards may be worth mentioning at some point, but remember they are only a feature. The benefit is that if the reader buys your product, they can rely on it.

You already know what your product or service's benefits are. That's what your readers need to know. Don't start by repeating what you've already told them in the headline. Keep their interest going with a steady flow of temptation – 'it's really light and easy to assemble . . . it's so well camouflaged you'll hardly know it's there . . . if you want to move it to another part of the garden, it's no problem . . .', and so on. Also, interest the readers with information they didn't know: 'The average garden climber grows four feet a year.'

If your customers are other businesses rather than the general public, there's a tendency to think you're writing your advertisement for a committee, or an office block, but in fact you're writing for a real person. Get a picture of them in your head, matching your target profile in terms of age, likely job title, disposable budget and so on. And remember that they're real – they probably hate getting up in the mornings, want to impress the boss, hope to come top of the sales league this month or whatever. So interest them with the benefits to them as well as to their company.

Tips for adding interest

There are several techniques you can use. Try some of these ideas:

- *use questions* for example, 'Would you like to tidy up your garden quickly and easily?'
- *repeat yourself* use the same word several times for impact: 'Easy to assemble, easy to move, easy to use . . . and easy on the pocket'
- *use pictures* cartoons are very popular, as are pictures of the product in use (photographs are more credible than drawings for this). If the product is very visual, such as a set of decorated china plates, you'll really have to use photographs

- *humour* this makes readers warm to you, but only if they find it funny – there's nothing worse than humour that falls flat. So keep it light, and check it with plenty of people you can trust to give you an honest opinion. And if in doubt – don't do it

- *people* testimonials – getting customers to say how good they've found your product – can be a good idea. But the best way to get quotes from customers is to write them yourself, and then ask the customer to put their name to them (you tell the customer that you're writing them to save them time and effort). If you want to offer them a choice of quotes, offer three. Make sure you'd be happy with any of them, but put your preferred one in the middle, as they'll usually go for the middle one. Make one of the others slightly weak, and the other slightly over the top. Choose a customer who fits your target profile. Don't invent testimonials.

Style

Follow the rules we set out in Chapter 4 for writing clear English: keeping your sentences short, avoiding jargon and so on. If you possibly can, address your reader as 'you'. Don't say, 'It saves 20 minutes of washing up a day', say, 'It will save *you* 20 minutes of washing up a day'.

You can get away with writing a lot about your product, if it's interesting and phrased from the reader's point of view. But don't cramp the text. White space is an important component of most advertisements. The more space there is around the headline or text, the more the eye will be drawn to it. It is also offputting to have to read small print; try to keep the text to 10 point or above. So if you want to write a lot, the answer is to use a bigger space.

Desire

Desire is not really a separate part of the advertisement, it is something you should nurture to grow out of the interest. But before your reader reaches the end of the advertisement (whether it's two lines or two pages long), they should want your product. So make sure you answer as many of their possible reservations as

143

you can in the space you've got. People put up barriers to deter themselves from spending money, such as 'I expect it's really expensive' or 'It probably takes six weeks to arrive'.

Your job is to remove all the potential barriers. They might be worrying about the price, so tell them what it is or at least let them know that it's cheaper than trellis, or it costs no more than the competition's products. They could be concerned about delivery or replacement parts or servicing or what happens if they want it in a different colour. Your research should have told you what people's biggest concerns are. Make sure you answer them, so that nothing stands in the way of your reader's desire for your product or service.

Action

Your reader is now slavering over your product. You grabbed their attention, you caught their interest, you've reassured them about every reservation they might have had, you've instilled in them a desire to buy it . . . so now what? Don't leave them hanging, tell them what they can do to bring themselves one step closer to owning your product:

- go to the shops and buy it (if it's easily available)
- call this number (Freephone numbers get a particularly high response) for a catalogue, appointment or whatever
- visit the showroom or offices
- pick up a brochure (tell them where from)
- return the coupon and we'll send you a brochure, visit you or whatever
- cut out the coupon and get 20% off your next purchase (coupons get a very good response, and they help you measure how effective your advertisement is. For business advertising, you get an even better response if you ask people to staple their business card to the coupon – this saves them having to write out their name and address).

Make sure the instructions are clear, and make it easy for people – let them use their credit card if possible. Don't use box numbers –

people seem to find them suspicious and are less likely to respond. And, of course, deal promptly with the responses.

Check that the advertisement meets the criteria

Once you've finished writing your advertisement, check it against the following list of questions (and ask someone else whose honesty you can trust to do the same) to make sure it meets the main criteria for a successful advertisement:

- Will your target readers see it?
- If they see it, will they read it?
- If they read it, will they understand it?
- If they understand it, will they believe it?
- If they believe it, will they act on it?

145

How will we know if it has worked?

Advertising can be an expensive business, however careful you've been, so you need to monitor its success to find out if it has been worth it. Otherwise, how will you know whether or not to do it again? You wouldn't believe how many businesses fail to do this but, fortunately, we can't afford to be that careless.

This is where the objective you defined earlier is so useful – that's the standard you're going to measure your advertisement's success against. However, suppose you decided that your objective was to generate 30 new enquiries and, in the last week, you had 90 enquiries? How can you tell how many of them were generated by your advertisement? Perhaps you got 30 more enquiries than usual, but maybe you put three advertisements in different magazines. How do you know which produced the best results?

It's a good idea to build identification codes into your advertisements to overcome this problem, for example:

- print a number on a tear-off coupon that differs with the

various publications, or different issues of the same publication, so you can identify the source of each coupon you receive

- if you advertise a phone number to call, use a dedicated extension number
- if you ask readers to write in, give them a fictitious name or department to write to so you can identify them
- whenever you take an enquiry, ask the caller where they heard of you (you've probably been on the receiving end of this one).

Keep thorough records of the responses you get to all the advertisements you place. Make a note of the following details:

- the number of responses
- nature of responses (enquiries, orders or whatever)
- 'conversion' rate (number of enquiries that you managed to turn into sales)
- general profile(s) of respondents
- the cost per response (total cost divided by the number of responses).

You'll also need to keep records of the advertisements themselves. Keep copies of each one, taking it from the publication it appeared in, and check whether or not:

- it appeared as you booked it, on the correct date
- it appeared in the position you specified (if you did)
- it appeared in a sensible place (if the publication's staff chose the position)
- any editorial nearby was relevant
- the quality of the printing – including colours, photographs and illustrations – was sufficient
- the coupon – if you included one – could be cut out (without cutting up something important on the back of it, like another coupon).

These points can make a difference to the response you get from the advertisement, so note down anything unfavourable or irregular, or particularly good, in your records. Then any comparisons you make with other issues or publications will be fairer.

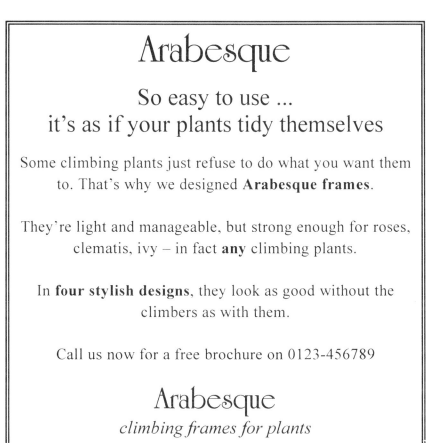

147

TESTING ADVERTISEMENTS

Do you reckon you should advertise inside the front cover of a magazine or inside the back cover? Which trade publication will you get the best response from? Would it be better to put an advertisement in a daily paper on a Tuesday or a Wednesday? You've come up with two headlines for your handbill – how do you know which will be best?

Which day you advertise or which headline you use could actually make a fair bit of difference. If you've done your research, you'll have narrowed down a lot of the options enormously, but you can't know everything. The answer is to test it. Some advertisements are one-offs, but a lot are repeated frequently. After all, if you get a response, why stop? All the research shows that repeating advertisements increases the response – people will say, 'I really need some new fencing. Hang on, where's the paper? There's that company that does unusual metal fencing – they're always in here somewhere . . .'. That's what you're after.

So it's worth making sure that your advertisement is in the best possible place. And you do that by trying it out in two or more ways and comparing the results. For example:

- place the advertisement in two different papers/magazines on the same day to compare the results from different papers
- place two different advertisements in the same paper/magazine on consecutive Tuesdays, consecutive monthly issues, and so on to compare the results from different advertisements. You might change only the headline or only the photograph
- place a smaller advertisement (to find out if you need to pay for the bigger one)
- move the advertisement to a different position (sometimes people get so used to a repeated advertisement that they stop seeing it. So it can help to move it occasionally)
- try a repeat advertisement in a different colour, or test two in different colours against each other
- try advertising more or less frequently, if you think this might affect the response.

In all these cases, monitor the effects of the alternatives, so you can find the best possible way to advertise.

So that's the nuts and bolts of advertising. It's that simple, and the trick is to keep it that way. Professional copywriters and art directors know when to break the rules, but we don't. So follow low cost marketing rule four: *keep it simple*. Most people go wrong by trying to be too clever. Just avoid gimmicks, stick to the rules and you'll be fine.

7

Direct mail

We haven't the money, so we've got to think.

Lord Rutherford

Direct marketing is any form of marketing that involves dealing directly with your customers rather than going through a retailer, agent, distributor or some other middle person. It includes advertisements that ask for a direct response, such as 'cut out the coupon' (which we looked at in the last chapter) and direct selling by telephone or face-to-face (which is dealt with in the next chapter). It also includes direct mail.

Direct mail is when you write directly to your customers and potential customers. This not only covers mail order, but also letters offering information, asking for appointments and so on. Many of the rules of research, advertising and other aspects of marketing can be applied to direct mail, so I shan't repeat them in detail here. But there are some additional factors and techniques to consider.

There are five main areas of direct mail to look at:

- planning the campaign
- putting together a mailing list
- what to say and how to say it
- getting your prospects to read it
- dealing with the response.

This chapter is not about how to become a direct mail expert – you could spend years learning exactly which is the best point size for typing the address on the envelope, or what colour paper to use if your prospects work in the medical profession. This chapter is simply about how to produce good direct mail material, at low cost, that will increase your response rate.

Planning the campaign

Remember rule three, *do it yourself*. There are agencies who will organise your direct mail campaign for you – find mailing lists, write the letters, design the envelopes, analyse the response – or there's the real world. Many of these agencies will do an excellent job, but if you can't afford it you're going to have to do it for yourself. And why not? You may well find that the response is as good at a fraction of the cost.

The first thing to do is to decide whether or not direct mail is a useful medium for you to sell your product or service. You might call it direct mail when you send it, but when you receive it you probably call most of it 'junk mail'. You need to be able to reach a well targeted readership who will regard your mailshot as interesting or useful, rather than something to be thrown in the nearest bin.

Direct mail is probably excellent for selling computer software upgrades to people who have bought software from you before. It's less useful for selling Lamborghinis to a randomly selected list of car owners. If you have a product for which you can target your potential customers closely, you are far more likely to be successful. Most of the wasted money in direct mail goes on not targeting accurately enough.

One of the great benefits of direct mail is that it's so easy to cost. You know before you start what it will cost you, in terms of:

- your time (with reasonable accuracy)
- printed materials (you can ask designers and printers for quotes)
- envelopes
- postage.

The only thing you don't know for certain is what response you'll get – in other words the income it will generate. But you can test a sample and then predict the future response rate. The more experienced you become, the less of a risk this will be.

Putting together a mailing list

There are several low cost ways in which you can obtain mailing lists:

- use your own customer list. This is by far the best list, as it's much more cost effective to sell to existing customers than to recruit new ones. The more information you have on your database the better, because then you can select only certain customers for some mailings – only company directors, for example, or only people who live in a certain postcode area, or have bought a particular product from you in the past

- create lists from the sources we listed in Chapter 2 (trade associations, directories, enterprise agencies, *Yellow Pages* and so on)

- swap lists with a non-competitive business in the same industry. For example, if you sell upholstery fabrics to retailers, get together with a company that sells haberdashery accessories (threads, needles and so on) and invite them to trade customer lists

- keep a scrapbook of cuttings, advertisements and articles that give details of potential customers. This may not give you thousands of leads, but it could give you dozens, and the better you get at it, the more productive the leads will be

- ask your own customers for referrals. If they're happy with you as a supplier, after all, why shouldn't they give you the names of other potential customers? This is particularly productive if you sell to businesses. Write to your long standing customers thanking them for their business, enclose a sheet with a few blank spaces for names and addresses, and ask them to fill it in and return it to you. You could even ask them to tick a box if it's OK for you to use their name. If you have a good relationship with your customers, you could get an excellent response from this – it's especially useful for getting customers in large organisations to suggest other potential customers in the same organisation. One point to note: thank them by letter for the referrals they give you, but don't cheapen the relationship by offering them any incentive for doing it.

Occasionally you may have to pay for a specialised list of contacts. If you are thinking about this, work out the costs and the expected response. If the value of a highly targeted list will offset the cost of renting it, then it's worth trying to find one. There are several places you can go if you want to rent a list:

- a mailing list broker (they are listed by the Direct Marketing Association – DMA – their address is given at the back of this book)
- *BRAD Direct Marketing* publish a directory of mailing lists that is updated every six months. (You should be able to find this at a good library and, likewise, the quarterly *Lists and Data Sources*)
- *Yellow Pages* will rent their lists of addresses, broken down into around 2000 business categories, or broken down by postcode (the address for their database is at the back of this book)
- some trade associations, professional associations and institutions, and Chambers of Trade and Commerce will rent lists of their members
- many magazines will rent out their subscriber lists.

Before you decide to pay for a list, however, there are a lot of points that it would be wise to check.

- *How accurate is it?* Find out what source the list was originally compiled from. Is this list of gardening enthusiasts made up of people who pay £15 a year to subscribe to a specialist gardening magazine or people who responded to a competition to win a free holiday advertised on a packet of compost? The more closely it matches your target profile, the more it's worth to you.
- *How up to date is it?* You don't want to pay 5 or 10 pence (which is the likely cost) per address if half the people on the list have moved since it was compiled.
- *How expensive is it?* You have to pay each time you use the list. It's not really worth trying to cheat, copying a rented list to use again – you could get caught. The list providers often include 'false' addresses so that if you re-use the list a copy of your

mailing will arrive through one of their letterboxes. Anyway, one mailing should bring you enough useful addresses of respondents to start your own list.

- *Does the list include names or just addresses or job titles?* The response will be better if the target's name is on the envelope. If the mailing is going to businesses, your target may never even see it if their name isn't on it – the receptionist may just bin it. For businesses use a job title as well, as people move on quite regularly. Then with any luck their successor will open it.

- *Can you test a sample?* You don't want to have to mail all 100 000 names in order to know if the mailshot will work – ask what the smallest sample you can test is. It's normally 5000, but you can ask for a special 'first time' deal.

- *Ask to see an example of the labels or envelopes.* Make sure they look attractive and won't put the readers off opening them.

- *Ask what responses to previous mailings from this list have been like* – but take the contents of the mailing into consideration.

By the way, I'm not going to go into the legal details, but don't forget that any stored data on living people is governed by the Data Protection Act, so it should be registered. If you want to know the guidelines, contact the Data Protection Registrar (see the address at the back of this book).

MAXIMISING YOUR CHANCES OF A GOOD RESPONSE

Some people are more likely to reply to direct mailshots than others, so lists of people who have replied in the past (this will include your own existing list of course) are more promising than others. This is true even if their only history of responding has been to different products from different companies.

You will also find that people who have failed to respond to you once might nevertheless reply next time you mail them. How often have you thought, 'I must reply to that/buy one of those/join that organisation/subscribe to that magazine', but you don't get round to it? A few weeks later, another mailshot arrives and you think, 'Oh yes, of course; I meant to do that – I'll do it this time.' Sometimes, in fact, it takes several reminders before you finally get round to it. And other people are reacting the same way to your mailshots.

One local charity was recruiting local businesses as corporate members. They mailed 10 000 companies, and 1% of them took out membership – 100 companies. Six months later, they sent out another mailing, to 5000 businesses this time. But they weren't new contacts; they were all businesses that had failed to respond the last time. Of these, 50 joined – 1% again. Six months later, they wrote to the same 5000 for the third time (excluding the ones who had joined of course). Once again, 50 of them took out membership subscriptions.

So if a mailing list is good and the response to it is good, it's worth writing again to the people who didn't respond the first time – they may just need reminding.

Merging and purging

According to research, 10% of all the responses to an average advertisement or offer are duplicated: the same person or company enquires twice, and is therefore listed twice. This means that if your list is made up of enquiries or you've rented a list made up in this way, 10% of the printing and mailing costs you are paying are wasted, and you can't afford that. So regularly *merge* duplicated addresses and *purge* the list of out-of-date addresses.

Not only will this save money, but it will placate your readers as well – many people (especially contributors to charities) get very irritated when they are sent two copies of the same information; not an attitude towards your company that you want to cultivate.

Mailing costs

Obviously, second class mail is cheaper than first. However, the Post Office will not guarantee to return undelivered letters unless you send them first class. You'll have to balance up the extra postage cost with the benefit of being able to clean up your mailing list when letters are returned unopened. Needless to say, they won't be returned anyway unless you put your return address on the envelope.

A return address can be very useful for cleaning your list, but it can also deter people from opening the letter. If you are mailing customers who know you, it's not likely to be a problem, but if you're mailing new contacts, it could put them off. If you're not sure, the best bet is to try half your mailshot with a return address and half without. See how many envelopes are returned, and how the response rate differs between the two halves of the mailing.

If you're mailing in bulk – anything from 4000 letters or 1000 packets upwards – it's worth checking out the Royal Mail's Mailsort service. They give a substantial discount on postage costs, and they guarantee to return anything that they can't deliver.

One other tip: there are ways of arranging for your mailshot to be posted in a foreign country where the postage costs are only a few pence per stamp. This often offsets the cost of sending the envelopes abroad to be posted, even for relatively small mailings. Your local Chamber of Commerce should have information on this. However, if you are selling expensive items to quality conscious customers, an Eastern European or Far East postmark may not give the best impression. Also, the system can be more trouble than it's worth, so investigate the alternatives and compare them.

What to say and how to say it

As with advertising, you need to start with rule one: *think*. What are you trying to achieve with this mailshot? Do you want direct orders from your mail-order catalogue, or are you trying to arrange appointments with potential customers? Or persuade regular customers to attend an event launching your new range? Before you sit down and write your letter, you need to know what it is asking the recipient to do.

The more the reader feels the letter is addressed to them, the more

155

likely you are to get a response. It helps enormously if you can call people by name. They are more likely to open the letter in the first place, and then more likely to read it.

By the same token, if you can let them know that this letter is written specially for people who have been customers for over five years, or people with gardens larger than an acre, they will feel you are really talking to them. You need to strike a balance here, though. Obviously you haven't got time to write individual letters to 5000 people, but could you write three letters – for people with small gardens, people with average size gardens and people with large gardens?

WHICH TYPE OF MAILSHOT?

Direct mailshots break down into two main categories – for want of better terminology, let's call them the hard sell and soft sell approaches. Hard sell is when you send out your mail-order catalogue to 80 000 people from a bought-in mailing list. Soft sell is when you write to your top 20 customers asking for an appointment to tell them about your new, top-of-the-range product. Obviously there is a huge range of possibilities between these two extremes, but nevertheless they all fit into one of these two approaches.

In a sense, the hard sell style is like a newspaper advertisement that goes direct to the customer, while the soft sell variety is like a telephone sales call that has been put in the post. If you had to communicate with your customers either through a newspaper or on the phone, which would you choose? It will depend on a lot of things – your objective, your relationship with the recipient, and your product or service. People expect a glossy, unpersonalised catalogue from their local stationery company, but they expect a personalised letter from their solicitor. If you think like a customer, it should be clear which style to use.

It's a good idea to spend a few weeks setting aside any 'junk' mail you get that you think is particularly good or particularly bad. Then look at them all and see what general lessons you can draw from them.

Hard sell

Even if you are sending a mail-order catalogue or a colour brochure, research indicates that your response will be higher if you send a letter with it. This type of mailshot is a form of advertising, and the letter should follow the format we looked at in the last chapter: AIDA – Attention, Interest, Desire, and Action. Of course, you will have more room than you might have wanted to pay for in an advertisement, but apart from the length the principle is the same.

Length

On the subject of length, remember who you're writing for. Busy managers don't have time to read long letters. But letters to home addresses can be longer. Either way, don't say more than you need to, and don't pad. The direct mail experts (those people we can't afford to pay) know how to write eight-page letters that keep you reading all the way – but we don't, so we won't risk trying.

157

Attention

I won't repeat Chapter 6, but here are some additional points about grabbing attention that apply to direct mail:

- don't forget how many unsolicited letters will arrive on your prospect's doormat on the same day as yours – you've got to make sure that yours is the one that stands out
- send something else with your letter – a free gift, a raffle ticket, a sample. We could send a free packet of sweet pea seeds, and suggest that the reader needs a climbing frame to support them as they grow. A recent survey in the US showed that 40% of the people who received free gifts could still remember the advertiser's name six months later, and 31% were still using the gift at least a year after receiving it
- persuade your readers to reply by offering something in exchange – the classic example is 'You have just won a free gift! To claim it, just return this form . . .'
- always put a headline at the top of the letter that includes a benefit to the reader
- provoke curiosity in the headline

- give special attention to the first sentence; for the mailshot to work, it must make them want to read the whole first paragraph. And the first paragraph must make them want to read everything else.

Interest

To hold the reader's interest:

- address the reader as 'you'
- as with an advertisement, you still need to focus on one main idea – probably your USP. In a letter, emphasise it three times
- remember you have more room to include testimonials than you do in an advertisement
- give any guarantees you can, especially a no-quibble money-back guarantee
- if you go over a page, finish the first page in the middle of a sentence so people have to turn over to finish the sentence.

Desire

To make readers want your product or service:

- as well as the points made in Chapter 6, you have more opportunity in a letter to stress the disadvantages of *not* buying. For example, 'The taller your climbing plants become, the more work it is to control them . . .'
- if you don't want an order, don't tell them everything. That is, if the objective is to get them to contact you for more information, don't give them all the information they want in the letter, or they'll have no reason to get in touch. Convince them they want to know more, but don't make them suspicious – if you don't tell them the price they'll assume it's really high (wouldn't you?). Hold back information such as which eight colours it comes in, or what the other five styles that aren't illustrated look like
- don't grovel – if your product is what they want, you're doing them as much of a favour by selling it to them as they are doing

you by buying it. So be polite and respectful, but don't demean yourself by 'humbly begging to be their obedient servant'.

Action

Now you have them wanting what you're selling, you must make it easy for them to order, preferably then and there:

- give them reasons to act straight away – limited stocks, pre-Christmas sale offer or whatever
- use a handwritten-style PS at the bottom of the letter to reiterate this: '　　　　　　　　　　　　　　　　　'
- make it very clear exactly what action people can take – call us, fill in the order form or whatever
- state your prices clearly.

159

SOFT SELL

These letters should *not* read like an advertisement. They should be highly targeted (like everything you do), but they should also be as personalised and friendly as possible. You will probably, but not necessarily, use them for smaller mailshots, and you might not even send a catalogue or brochure with them. They are often the better option for products that have a high price or high quality image.

There is (yes, you've guessed it) a formula to remember for this kind of letter; the mnemonic for it is SCRAP, which stands for Situation, Complication, Resolution, Action, Politeness.

- *Situation* Start by stating the position that the customer or the market is in at the moment, but don't state the obvious or tell them something they already know. Tell them something like, 'Half a million people every year buy a computer for the first time.'
- *Complication* Now tell them the problem associated with this: 'The majority of them spend up to £1000 more than they need to.'

- *Resolution* Tell them that you can sort the problem out, explaining how: 'Our new guide, *Buying Your First PC*, will steer you through the pitfalls . . .'

- *Action* So what do you want them to do about it? 'Fill in the enclosed order form and return it to us.'

- *Politeness* Just round the letter off pleasantly: 'We look forward to hearing from you.'

The letter needs to be a little longer than this, of course, but those are the basic ingredients. You still need to include the obvious selling points – the USP, the benefits, any guarantees and so on. Here are a few more points to remember:

- if you are sending these letters to existing customers in small enough numbers, you could even catch their attention by faxing the letter

- you still need to start with an attention grabbing headline

- people are always impressed if you tell them interesting facts they didn't know about their business or market

- you can still send tickets, samples or free gifts

- you can still tell them that stocks are running low or the offer only runs until the end of the month

- remember not to grovel – if they will arrange an appointment you'll be 'delighted' or 'very happy to meet them', but there's no need to be 'deeply grateful'. This type of phrase implies that *they* have nothing to gain from it

- when it comes to the 'action' it is a good idea to leave the ball in your own court if you can. So, if you're only mailing 20 people to invite them to a product launch, tell them that *you'll* contact *them* to see if they can make it. That way, you retain control.

Here's an example of a soft sell letter targeted at people with small gardens whose addresses have urban postcodes.

Dear Mr Potter

**Your garden can look as interesting in winter
as it does in summer**

Like most gardeners, you will have noticed the increasing
popularity of climbing plants – roses, clematis, honeysuckle,
jasmine, and many other less common varieties. Their
popularity isn't surprising; you can increase the amount of
colour and greenery tremendously when you use vertical as well
as horizontal space. And in our ever more crowded towns and
cities, climbing plants also provide the perfect screening from
neighbours and passers-by.

But there's a snag. Climbing plants need support, and after
the flowers have died and the leaves have fallen you can spend
half the year looking at bare and unattractive scaffolding.

It is to overcome this problem that we have developed
Arabesque climbing frames. They are sturdy and weatherproof
and give your climbers all the support they need through the
spring and summer. But, autumn reveals not bare scaffolding,
but attractive and elegant tracery that gives interest and focus to
the garden throughout the winter months.

The two enclosed tickets give you free admission to the
Romchester Gardening Show on 30 March (usual price £2.00),
where you can have a look at our full range of fencing and
free-standing frames. What's more, we'll give you a free
clematis to take home with you if you place an order at the
exhibition.

In the meantime, if you would like to see our full brochure,
please return the enclosed form and we'll send you a copy
straight away.

I look forward to meeting you.

Yours sincerely,

Robin Jones

Robin Jones
Managing Director, Arabesque

161

Getting your prospects to read it

You need to think about the packaging of your mailshot as well as the contents. The envelope is an important part of it – it's the first thing your readers see, after all. Again, it's back to rule one: *think*. Think like a customer – how would you feel if this envelope landed on your doormat? Would you read it?

THE ENVELOPE

- Bear in mind what we said in Chapters 4 and 5 about consistency of image. Your envelopes should fit in with your corporate style as well as the letter or brochures inside it.

- You could trail the contents on the outside of the envelope – the classic is 'Inside . . . your chance to win a free gift!' This can arouse curiosity and interest and encourage people to open it.

- You could keep the contents secret if you think your customers will be put off by 'junk mail'. Business customers in particular may be deterred.

- A high quality envelope can give the impression that what it contains is important – you may find that this increases the response sufficiently to justify the extra cost.

- Does the style of the envelope fit in with the message you are sending? If the letter inside is personalised, the envelope should be too. If you are enclosing a bright, exciting catalogue or brochure, use a bright, exciting envelope – it doesn't have to be white or brown.

- Some companies use special devices to get people to open the envelope – such as making it look like a bill. This can work, but don't forget to consider how people might feel when they realise they've been 'conned' into opening it.

- If you're enclosing a free gift, say so on the envelope.

- Maybe you don't want to use an envelope at all? I recently received a postcard from a supplier, with the message printed in a script typeface so it looked handwritten. It was so catchy, I couldn't resist reading it – and I usually throw junk mail away without even opening it.

Apart from the basic contents of the mailshot, there are certain factors that increase the response you get from direct mail, as shown by research over the years. Some of them are, quite frankly, unfathomable – but they work.

PRESENTATION

- Use good quality paper and print on to it – don't send out tatty photocopies.
- Use plenty of white space (we looked at the value of this in Chapter 4).
- Vary the layout of your letter with subheadings, bullet points, underlined phrases, words in bold.
- Indent the first line of each paragraph.
- Don't justify the right-hand margin (that is, don't instruct the word processor to line up the right-hand ends of the lines).
- Use illustrations – tables, charts, line drawings – to make the page look more interesting.
- Add a PS, in a 'handwritten' typeface, under the signature.
- Bear in mind the way people's eyes move around a page, and plan the layout so your readers see what you want them to first (see illustration overleaf).

163

COLOUR

- Use a second colour if you can afford it, to highlight important headlines and key phrases in the main copy.
- If the other colour is black, the eye will be drawn to even a small area of colour on the page, so make sure you colour the things you most want the reader to look at.
- If you use too much colour, however, you start to dilute the effect.
- Soft, earthy colours are peaceful and convey honesty. Bright colours engender excitement.

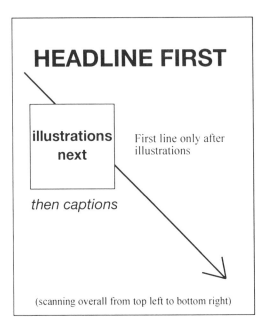

HEADLINE FIRST

illustrations next

First line only after illustrations

then captions

(scanning overall from top left to bottom right)

OTHER INCLUSIONS

If you are sending out a mail-order catalogue or brochure, you should include a separate order form and a return envelope, as well as your letter and the catalogue.

Order form

- Design this in the same style as the letter and brochure, and use paper of equal quality.
- Make the instructions very clear.
- Don't forget that you will need to work from this order form, so it must be easy for you and your staff to follow as well.
- Make it as easy as possible by giving customers boxes to tick.
- Allow a column for customers to put the number of items they want – make it as easy as possible for them to order, say, three of the same thing.
- Restate any offers or bargains on the order form.

- Print the address on the order form in case the customer loses the rest of your material.
- Code the order form so you can keep full records of the source of the order and so on.

Return envelope

- Don't waste too much money on the cost of these, unless you are going for a seriously high-class image.
- Make the envelope reply-paid.
- You could send a reply-paid card, with boxes to tick asking for more information or a free trial.

Dealing with the responses

An average response rate to an unsolicited mailing is usually quoted as being about 1–2%. But in fact it varies widely according to the accuracy of the list, the nature of the product and the quality of the material that is mailed. Occasionally it can get up to 10 or 15%, but above this would be very rare.

Make sure you can cope with the response. If you're mailing 5000 people with a special bargain offer, make sure you have the product in stock when the replies start to come in. If this is going to be a problem, stagger the mailing over several days or weeks. Equally, if you have said that you will telephone in the next few days, or call round, make sure you do.

If you costed the mailing before you started, the important thing is that it should pay for itself. Over time you can test different mailshots, different market sectors or mailing at different times of year to find out which gives you the best response, along the same lines as the advertisement testing discussed in Chapter 6.

Keep testing mailshots against each other to find out where and when you can get your best results. Direct mail is a growing medium, and one that can be highly cost effective. The key to minimising your costs and maximising your profit is to target as tightly as you can.

8

Selling

One of the best ways to persuade others is with your ears – by listening to them.

Dean Rusk

Selling is the bottom line of marketing. Everything else you do – from planning to advertising – is wasted if you don't sell your product or service at the end of it. And of course the better you are at selling, the lower your costs: selling is an expensive business in terms of time, administration, paperwork, petrol, free samples and all the rest of it. So the better your 'hit rate', the better this money is targeted and the less of it is wasted.

Even if you employ skilled sales staff, you still need to know how to sell. The more time you spend with customers and potential customers, finding out what they like about your product or service and what their objections are, the more low cost research you'll find yourself doing.

There are all kinds of different ways of selling your product, such as:

- face-to-face
- over the telephone
- presentations
- exhibitions
- product demonstrations.

This chapter looks at the specific guidelines for each of these, but they all follow the same basic principles, so we'll start by looking at the underlying rules of selling.

The basics of selling

MAKING CONTACT

You can't sell anything to anyone until you're communicating with them, so the first thing you have to do is to strike up a dialogue. If you've been selling to the same regular customer for years, it's easy to do. But what if you're chasing up a new lead? You want to speak to the prospect in order to sell to them, or make an appointment, or arrange a presentation.

If you just turn up at someone's door without an appointment, you are unlikely to get very far. What's more, it's a very expensive way of going about things – all that petrol, all that time spent travelling. It's better to phone first, whether you are aiming for a telephone conversation or a face-to-face appointment.

167

If you can sell your product as effectively over the phone as face-to-face, it's better to do so over the phone because it's far cheaper, and you can speak to more people in a day. However, some products need to be sold face-to-face, including most products that:

- the customer needs to see
- they are spending a lot of money on.

If you have a product that you could sell face-to-face, such as traditional carpets, it's usually a good idea to choose this option if your brand has a prestigious image, to set you apart from your lower quality competitors and to make the customer feel important.

Before you speak to a business customer, you need to know their name. If you don't already have this, ask the receptionist. You will have a pretty good idea of who you usually sell to in any organisation – production managers, chief buyers or whatever – so ask the receptionist to give you the appropriate name.

Once you've found out who you need to deal with, either ask to speak to them or make an appointment to talk to them. You can make telephone appointments – to phone someone at an arranged time – as well as appointments to visit. Remember at this point that you're not trying to sell the product, you're trying to sell *the idea of making an appointment* to discuss the product. Start this conversation by:

- calling the person by name (for example, 'Good morning, Mr Smith')
- introducing yourself and your company ('I'm Robin Jones of Arabesque')
- giving them a reason to want to know more ('I'm calling about our frames for growing climbing plants so that they look stylish and tidy without any hard work').

The reason you give them for wanting to know more should include a strong benefit to them (remember the points about describing benefits not features in Chapters 4 and 6).

168

Getting past the secretary

When you come up against this problem, the first thing is to know the name of the person you want to speak to. The secretary, assistant or whoever screens their calls will be more likely to co-operate with you. If they say that the person you want to speak to is unavailable, ask when would be a good time to phone them. The secretary cannot very well refuse to answer. Ask them to narrow it down to a particular time of day, then say, 'Thank you, I'll make a note in my diary to call back at 3.30 on Wednesday. I'll speak to you then.' When you call back on Wednesday, it will be hard not to put you through as they effectively gave you an appointment to call. When you ring back you can say, 'Hello, it's Robin Jones here. You asked me to call back now to speak to Mr Smith.'

It's never worth being rude to a secretary or assistant. You need them on your side. The better they like you, the more inclined they will be to help you speak to the person you want to. So always be polite and friendly, and don't take it out on them if Mr Smith never seems to be there.

THE SALES APPOINTMENT

Research the customer

The more you know about your customer, the better chance you have of selling to them. If you know they're expanding their fleet of lorries, closing down one of their branches or launching a new product, you can find benefits of buying your product that link to these factors: 'Of course, now that you're moving another 50 staff to this office you'll be extending the car park. Have you thought about how you're going to screen the cars from the reception area?'

The other reason for researching the customer is so that you don't make a fool of yourself:

You: 'So would you like to order another five plants to train over your new fencing?'
Customer: 'Are you kidding? The last five died within a week. We've been on to your people four times in the last fortnight and they still haven't done anything.'

There are three key areas you need to research:

- *the customer* know where the person you deal with fits into the organisation, what their remit is, and if it changes. And learn everything you can about their company – read the trade press, their literature, their competitors' catalogues and so on

- *the product* you should be able to answer every question possible from your customers, and fill them in on new services, additional lines and how they can get the best from your products

- *the relationship between your organisation and theirs* don't make a fool of yourself – you need to know what this customer usually buys from you, what they've tried in the past, and whether there have been any problems regarding quality, delivery, accounts procedures or anything else.

Setting objectives

Before you start trying to sell – over the phone or face-to-face – you need to set an objective. What are you actually trying to achieve? If you sell chocolate bars to sweet shops, you probably want to sell about 50 on your first visit to a new customer. If, on the other hand, you sell aircraft carriers to government ministries, you'll be aiming for your first visit to lead to setting a date for the next meeting with someone more senior, or perhaps a presentation. You don't expect a junior minister at a first meeting to say, 'Sounds great. We could probably do with a few more aircraft carriers; we'll take half a dozen.'

So you need to set a realistic objective, but you also need a fallback position. Otherwise, you don't know what to aim for if you don't meet your first goal. What you should end up with is what's known as a 'hierarchy of objectives', which will look something like this:

1 Sell half a dozen plant frames
2 Sell three plant frames
3 Sell one plant frame
4 Sell one frame on sale or return
5 Persuade the customer to put leaflets about plant frames on their sales counter
6 Get the customer to agree to visit next month's demonstration.

Listening to the customer

Remember we looked at the difference between features and benefits earlier? Well, the same feature can have different benefits to different customers. You've got to find out which benefits *this* customer is interested in. And you do that by listening to them. Otherwise, you could spend hours plugging the fact that your product is inexpensive without having learned that your customer is a multi-millionaire who is actually far more interested in the fact that it's available in purple.

Ask open questions
For the first three-quarters of the conversation, you want the

customer to do about three-quarters of the talking. Draw them out. Encourage them to tell you what they really want from the product, what benefits they're looking for. One of the best techniques for doing this is to ask open questions. These are questions to which the customer cannot simply answer 'Yes', 'No' or 'Last Friday'. Open questions need longer answers; for example, 'How do you decide which plant frames and trellises to stock?' Open questions usually start:

- 'How . . .?'
- 'What . . .?'
- 'Why . . .?'

Starting a question with 'Why . . .?' can sometimes sound slightly pushy and rude. You can always rephrase it to 'For what reason . . .?', 'What is the thinking behind . . .?', 'What has made you take that view?'

171

Show you're listening

Write down the answers. For one thing, you may think you'll remember, but after you've spoken to another half dozen people you may well forget which one is which. In a face-to-face interview, however, it helps because it makes the customer feel important. For the same reason, show that you're listening. Make listening noises, and repeat key phrases back to them:

Customer: 'We reorganised our whole production schedule, and now we need all our supplies delivered by Tuesday lunchtime.'
Salesperson (writing it down): 'Ah, Tuesday lunchtime.'

Always try to refer back to something the customer said earlier when you introduce a new question, for example, 'You were saying you've reorganised your production schedule – will that mean larger quantities?'

Handling objections

Wouldn't it be great if customers and prospects always finished a sales interview by saying, 'Your product sounds wonderful. Can I have ten?' But they don't. They say irritating things like, 'Mmm, it sounds a bit pricey', and, 'I'm not sure my boss will think we need it.' So how do you get over these objections?

Ask them to be specific
The first thing you need to do is to ask the customer to make the objection specific. You can say something like, 'How much were you expecting to pay?', or, 'What would worry your boss about it?'

Put the objection in context
Once you know exactly what the problem area is, put it into context for the customer; show them why it's not as expensive as they think, or why delivery doesn't have to be a problem, or whatever it is they're objecting to. For example, 'Well, don't forget that delivery and installation are included in the price, and there's a year's guarantee so you won't have to spend anything more for the next 12 months.'

172

Give compensations
As well as putting it into context, offer other compensating factors, related to the objection and unrelated, such as, 'It lasts twice as long as cheaper versions (related to cost objection) and it will help to streamline your production line and improve health and safety standards (unrelated).' Customers often need to be reassured that they're making the right decision, especially with high price items. They want to hear you tell them that their boss will be impressed with them, their living room will look beautiful or they'll really appreciate the extra power and safety of this model of car.

Bear in mind, when it comes to objections, that many people who *want* to buy your product will object nevertheless. They're worried that when they talk to their boss, their partner or whoever else is involved in the buying decision, the other person will object; they want to furnish themselves with answers to these anticipated objections. So they're getting you to supply them.

Closing the sale
This is the bit we all really hate because we risk rejection. Of

course, rationally, we know they're rejecting our product or service, not us. But we still don't like it. However, if you're selling on a budget you can't afford *not* to take the risk. And as early in the conversation as you can – that way you can fit in more calls and, hopefully, more sales before the end of the day.

Recognise buying signals

You don't want to be pushy, so how do you know when to try to close? The answer is when the customer signals that they want to buy. Don't wait for them to say, 'Please can I buy one?' because they may not say it for hours. A buying signal is a sign of approval of the product, preferably related to their own need for it. Here are some examples of buying signals:

- 'I could certainly do with something to keep my roses tidier'
- 'That seems a fair price'
- 'You have a 48-hour delivery time? That's very good'
- 'You know, you're the first people I've found who do it in purple'.

173

Close the sale

Once you hear one of these signals, it's time to move in for the close. There are hundreds of different ways of closing the sale, but they are all different ways of doing the same thing: asking for the order. In fact, it's quite reasonable to do exactly that – 'Would you like to order one?' – but there are numerous ways to ask for the order indirectly. Here are a few of the ones most commonly used.

- *The assumptive close* You simply take the order without ever asking them directly, for example, 'I'll order one for you today, then it'll be delivered before next Friday.'
- *The alternative close* Offer them a choice so that whichever option they choose is an order. 'Shall I put you down for four or six?', 'Would you prefer it in light purple or dark purple?'
- *The order form close* When the buying signals start, get out your order form and, without comment, start filling it in. Ask the questions on the form, such as, 'So you'd want the model with the four inch diameter tubing?' and work your way

through. When you get to the end, they have effectively ordered, and you simply have to say, 'Could you give me the order number, please?' Don't say, 'Sign this please', say, 'Would you like to OK this?'

- *The question close* Answer a question with a question, such as, 'Would you be able to deliver it on Saturday morning?' Your reply is 'Would you like us to deliver it on Saturday morning?' If they say 'Yes', they've bought it.

- *The puppydog close* This operates on the principle that once they've got used to the product or service, they won't want to be without it. It goes something along the lines of 'Why don't I leave it with you for a week, then see if you want to keep it after that. If not, we'll take it back and we won't charge you.' This is the principle that a lot of book clubs work on: 'Keep it for ten days' free trial' – of course, hardly anyone returns the books after that.

One last point about closing the sale: if someone is clearly *not* going to buy, get out as fast (and politely) as you can. Don't waste time (and money) flogging a dead horse – you can't afford to. Knowing when to give up is one of the greatest skills of low cost selling.

The sales appointment checklist

1 Research the customer.
2 Set objectives.
3 Listen to the customer.
   - Ask open questions.
   - Show you're listening.
4 Handle their objections.
   - Ask them to be specific.
   - Put the objection in context.
   - Give compensations.
5 Close the sale.
   - Recognise buying signals.
   - Close the sale.

NEGOTIATING

There are several books about negotiating and if it's something you have to do often, you should read them and, perhaps, enrol on a training course as well if you can afford to. Spending on a good course will be money well invested. Negotiating skills are important to low cost marketing because they can make a substantial difference to the value of the deals you strike with your customers. Good negotiating can save you a fortune and cost nothing.

Many people think of negotiating as an occasional skill, that is, one you don't need often enough to train thoroughly in. But once in a while you could really save some money if you knew what you were doing. In any case, the basic skills apply just as much to getting the best price out of an advertising salesperson as they do to arranging complex international deals. So it's worth going through the central techniques, which underlie all the others.

Psychology

Negotiation relies heavily on the use of psychology. It's important not to let the other side know what you would be prepared to settle for, or there's no chance you'll get more than that out of them. So you need to be quite poker-faced about the process. However, don't forget that you are dealing with customers, and you don't want to damage your relationship with them in the long term. It's quite possible to be firm and give nothing away, yet still keep smiling all the time. In fact, it can lull the other side into a false sense of security. So resist the temptation to show your annoyance or frustration with them.

People tend to come away from negotiations feeling they have 'won' or 'lost'. Most people are reluctant to conclude a deal until they think it is a 'win' for them. Take advantage of this – let the other side think they've won. It's no skin off your nose – you know you've got what you wanted – but let them *think* they drove a hard bargain and got more out of you than you meant to give.

If you decided from the start that it's not a problem to deliver within a fortnight, don't tell them that. Say, 'Well, I suppose if you can pay within 30 days instead of 60 we could find a way to deliver in two weeks. I'll have to double-check with production of course, but I think we can guarantee it.' They think they've negotiated you into a corner but, in fact, you were planning to deliver that fast anyway. Meanwhile, you've got them to agree to pay within 30 days instead of 60. Everybody's happy.

The four rules of negotiating

These are:

- aim high
- get them to put their complete shopping list on the table before you start
- make trade-offs, not concessions
- find all the variables you can.

Aim high

You won't get anything if you don't ask for it. Before an important negotiation, talk yourself into asking for as much as you can. A freelance was once asked to quote for a job when he was just starting out. He wondered if he could get away with quoting £500. After a day or so, he'd persuaded himself he could ask for £750. After all, they could always haggle him down if they wanted to. By the end of the week he was wondering if he mightn't get away with asking for £1000?

Eventually he met the customer again, who asked him what he'd charge for the job. He took a deep breath and said, 'Fifteen hundred pounds'. The customer replied, 'OK, that's fine. Now, let's talk about the delivery time . . .'. He could almost certainly have asked for more, but if he hadn't talked himself up over a couple of weeks, he'd have been struggling to do the job for £500. If you ask too much, they'll negotiate you down. But if you don't ask enough, you'll never be able to push the price up later.

If you do negotiate down, though, give a reason for dropping your price, for example, 'Well, if the initial proposal was only for a telephone call and not a typed report, I suppose . . .'.

Get them to put their complete shopping list on the table before you start

The point about negotiations is that there are a lot of factors involved and they must all balance each other in some way in order to make a deal. So if the price is higher than you wanted, the payment terms need to be better; if the colour range isn't what you'd hoped, the delivery should be quicker to compensate.

You need to know what all the relevant factors are before you start, so you don't have to agree anything until you know what else is balancing it. Once you've said 'Yes' to the price, you can no longer use it as a lever for easing the payment terms. So get the other side to reveal all their requirements before you begin to discuss any of them. Then you can keep them all in balance.

Make trade-offs, not concessions

Suppose you're convinced that they won't go for the deal unless you drop the price. Secretly you know you could afford to bring it down to a level they find affordable. But don't just concede the point – trade it. Agree to give them a discount if they'll yield something in return – slower delivery, no customised products, faster payment or whatever.

Find all the variables you can

The obvious factors for negotiation are price, delivery time and payment terms. But keep looking for other trade-offs. For example, if you're buying a house, you might agree a certain price on condition that they leave all the curtains; if you're negotiating your salary in a new job, you might agree a certain sum on condition that they increase the holiday allowance or sponsor your MBA.

177

Customer care

People are more likely to buy from you if they like you, and good customer care is free. Moreover, it is far cheaper to hang on to the customers you already have than to incur the cost of recruiting new ones. Of course, you need the new ones as well, but you want to fund the search for them from the profits you make from your regular customers.

Whatever your customers expect of you, do more. If you say you'll call them back within 20 minutes, call them back within 10. If they walk into your reception area unexpectedly, show you recognise them by calling them by their name. The key is to ask yourself two questions every time you deal with a customer:

1 'What does this customer want?'
2 'What extra can I do that they aren't expecting?'

If you give them what they want, they'll be satisfied. If you give them something extra, they'll remember you and be far more likely to choose your company over your competitors in future. Here are a few tips for achieving professional customer care:

- always do what you say you will (and go one better if you can)
- always greet them with a smile (even on the phone) and call them by name
- offer them coffee or tea as soon as they arrive in your reception, office or shop
- compliment them – not in the sense of empty flattery, but if you genuinely like their management style, their earrings or their new advertising campaign, say so
- remember personal details – they took their driving test last Wednesday, they always go to Crete on holiday, they can't stand meetings on Friday afternoons and so on
- if they want your product or service for something special – the opening of their new plant, a wedding, a new system being installed, a trade show – phone and ask them how the event went.

HANDLING COMPLAINTS

Even the best run companies receive the occasional complaint. It may not be your fault, but if the customer thinks it is, it needs sorting out. Don't despair when a customer complains, however, because if you handle it properly, they are actually *more* likely to buy from you again than if they'd never had a complaint. The attitude you want to generate in them is, 'Everybody's human, and at least with this company if something goes wrong, they get it sorted out quickly and properly.' Bear in mind the seven key steps for handling complaints.

1 *Listen* For one thing, you can't sort the problem out properly until you understand exactly what it is. But even if you're certain you know, the customer still needs to get their frustration, anger or whatever emotion they're feeling, off their chest. If they feel you're not listening, they will get angrier (wouldn't you?).

2 *Sympathise* This is not the same thing as apologising. You can say you're sorry to hear that their fencing fell down without saying that it was your fault. Customers are often 'defensively angry' – they're frightened you'll blame them for the fault or say there's nothing to complain about. So thank them for bringing it to your attention as quickly as you can. The rule for apologising is simple: *always* apologise if you're sure it's your fault; *never* apologise if it's not your fault.

3 *Don't justify* Once the customer has calmed down, the object of the exercise is to solve their problem, not conduct a post mortem into how it happened. They will not feel happier if you say, 'It's not our fault, you must have put the fencing up the wrong way.' There's no need to allocate blame at all, especially if you think they are responsible for the problem. Even if they ask why it happened, don't justify. Just say, 'I can't say for sure at the moment, but the important thing is to put it right or get you a replacement as quickly as we can.'

4 *Identify the options* If there is a fault with the fencing, for example, you could replace it, send someone round to fix it or give the customer a refund or a credit note. With other complaints there are other options, of course.

5 *Find a solution* What the customer really wants is a solution. They may also have needed to let off steam but, in the end, they came and complained because they wanted the problem fixed. As long as they are in a reasonable mood by this stage (which will depend on how you have treated them), they will want to resolve

the problem as much as you do. Tell them which options you can see, and ask them what they would like you to do to put things right. Always give them a choice – make it their decision, not yours. Often the answer will be easier, more reasonable and less demanding than you imagined.

6 *Take action* Carry out whatever solution you have agreed, and make doubly sure it all goes to plan.

7 *Follow up* Contact the customer after you have carried out the repair, replaced the goods or whatever, and make sure they are now happy with everything.

In the average business, 96% of unhappy customers don't complain – most of them simply don't come back – but they complain to their friends. So when one of your customers does let you know that they're not happy, you want to grab the chance to put things right.

Other approaches to selling

TELESALES

The groundrules for selling apply just as much to telesales as they do to face-to-face selling. However, there are a few extra things to consider:

- people find it far easier to terminate a phone call than they do a face-to-face meeting, so you have to work even harder to hold their interest. Try hooking people into conversation by saying something about them or their company, such as, 'I notice you're taking on 50 extra staff . . .', or, 'You must be getting busy with Christmas coming up . . .'

- because the customer can't see you, you have to put all your body language into your voice. You can't step forward confidently and shake their hand warmly, so you'll have to speak with confidence and have a friendly smile in your voice instead

- you need to be extra careful not to mumble or gabble. They might work out the gist face-to-face, but on the phone they could just have missed one of your key selling points

■ when your customer can't see you, you have to make it even more obvious that you're listening to them, which can simply mean saying 'Mmm', but you should also repeat back key phrases.

PRESENTATIONS

Car manufacturers present their newest models amid flashing lights, smoke, dry ice and live music. But for most of us a presentation that costs almost nothing will be just as successful in selling our product or service, just so long as we follow the basic rules. The skills of presenting really fall into two areas: preparing for the presentation, and delivering it.

Preparing for the presentation

Rule one of low cost marketing is vital here: *think*. You can't afford to impress your customers with dry ice and fireworks, so you'll have to impress them with facts and benefits instead. If you plan carefully, you can work out what to say and how to say it in the clearest and most convincing way. The following guidelines will help you do this.

1 *Research* Find out all about the audience. What their level of knowledge is, their attitude to your product and their knowledge of it, their past experiences and their future needs.

2 *Collate the information* Collect all the facts that this group of people will need (do they need the basics explained or are they technical people who will want a lot of detail?). Decide which detailed information would be better handed out afterwards in an information pack, and which statistics should be presented as charts.

3 *Structure the presentation* Here is a very useful four part structure to base it on.
- ■ *Position* Outline the current situation: 'You have 50 staff who travel to work by car and use the car park at the front of the building.'
- ■ *Problem* Explain why the situation needs to change: 'The

reception area overlooks the car park, and so does the dining room, where important visitors are entertained. The unattractive view isn't really in keeping with the smart, high quality image of the company.'

- *Possibilities* Put forward the options: 'You could move the car park, you could build a solid structure, or you could erect screen fencing that you could train plants over.'
- *Proposal* Explain which option you recommend, and why: 'Moving the car park would be very expensive, building a solid wall or slatted fence could be expensive and would certainly look stark; it wouldn't be much of an improvement on overlooking the car park. So the best option would be Arabesque fencing, which is relatively inexpensive and not only obscures the view of the car park but also creates an attractive outlook over low maintenance plants, such as clematis and climbing roses.'

4 *Write your notes* Prepare notes to talk from; it comes across far better than reading out a full script. Put subject headings on your note cards, and add key phrases that you want to remember as well. When it comes to the introduction, however, write this out (writing as you would speak, not in formal written English) and memorise it.

5 *Rehearse* Rehearse on your own, rehearse in front of a mirror, rehearse with colleagues; just keep rehearsing until you know it backwards and not even a major attack of nerves can throw you off course.

Delivering the presentation

1 Start with a smile and a friendly introduction.
2 Follow the rules in Chapter 4 for writing English – they apply to speaking it as well:
    - avoid jargon
    - use short words and short sentences
    - use active, not passive, verbs
    - use concrete rather than abstract nouns.
3 Don't mumble or gabble. Remember that adrenalin affects your sense of time, so what seems like an interminable pause to you

is hardly noticeable to your audience.

4 Make eye contact with everyone in the audience.

The more complicated and clever you try to make your present-ation, the more pitfalls you are digging for yourself. Remember rule four – *keep it simple*. Your customers only want to know two things:

- what your product can do for them
- whether it will be worth more than it will cost (in terms of effort, time and so on, as well as money).

If you can satisfy them on these two points, you've done as much as any amount of fireworks and showiness would do.

Most people suffer from nerves, at least to some extent, when giving a presentation. There are lots of different relaxation and visualisation techniques for dealing with this, so if you find one that works for you, use it. Quite honestly, though, the single best cure for nerves is confidence – the better you know what you're doing and the more thoroughly you've rehearsed, the less nervous you will feel.

183

EXHIBITIONS

The single biggest (and most expensive) mistake people make in exhibiting is to take a stand at the wrong exhibition. Exhibitions aren't cheap – a well placed stand can generate far more than it costs, but a badly selected trade show or exhibition can be a stupendous waste of money. There are plenty of good reasons for exhibiting, but 'to show the flag' or 'because we always have' aren't among them. Nevertheless, they're the most common rea-sons you hear. So the first thing to do is to decide whether or not to exhibit, and if so, where.

Trade shows tend to be open to businesses only, so the visitors are mostly customers and potential customers. There are more than 3000 trade shows held in this country each year, at venues from Earl's Court and the NEC to your local hotel. They are publicised in advance in the monthly *Exhibition Bulletin* (address at the back of the book). You need to find out if a promising looking show in your field is really going to bring you enough business to be worth attending. So here are a few tips:

- visit the show if you're uncertain, and wait until next year to exhibit if you decide it looks right

- be wary of new shows; in general, give them a couple of years to get going, then see what you think

- ask to see last year's catalogue so you can find out who exhibited. You could ring any of last year's visitors who aren't competitors and ask them whether it was successful

- ask the organisers to let you know who has booked space for this year's show already

- ask for a visitor breakdown of last year's show – the important thing is quality, not quantity of visitors, so if most of your customers are production managers, it won't help to go to a show where all the visitors are marketing directors. It would be better to attend a show that had only 50 visitors in a week so long as they were all production managers.

Work out the cost and likely income for each show (based on the organiser's figures of last year's visitors). The costs will include the space, the stand, display materials, especially printed literature, advertising your presence at the show, staff time, travel, food and accommodation. A good show can generate enough to cover this and plenty more, but make sure you're choosing the right exhibition before you sign on the dotted line.

Exhibition stand technique

If you've never done this before, be warned – it's more exhausting than you can imagine, and you need to appear constantly fresh and welcoming to your customers and prospects. Here's a rundown of the main points to consider:

- *Encourage people to the stand* Be aware of how you are positioned. If several of you huddle in a clump in the corner of the stand, no-one will want to break up the clique. If you stand on the front edge with your arms folded, no-one will dare pass. Always look welcoming, and don't make people feel you'll accost them as soon as you see them.

- *Identify visitors* Give people a few moments to look around when they reach the stand – don't hover around them. If they're serious visitors, they won't run away. Then start a conversation. Don't ask, 'Can I help you?' as they may well say 'No'. Try open questions, such as 'What sort of climbing plants do you have?', or, 'How do you control your plants at the moment?' As soon as you can, ask the visitor's identity. Exhibition stands are busy places, and if the visitor turns out not to be a potential customer, you haven't got time to stand around chatting. Be polite, but move on as fast as you can. Remember that everyone who comes to your stand could be a competitor until you've found out otherwise, but if this is someone who might want to do business with you, you need to know who they are in order to follow up the conversation later.

- *Keep records* Keep a log of all the visitors who might bring you business. Note down their details, any literature you gave them, and what follow-up action you need to take. Make sure everyone in your team is aware of the potential value of this record book, and don't let it get lost.

- *Follow up* You wouldn't believe how many people don't do this. However, we can't afford to miss an opportunity like this: these are all promising leads – that's why we went to the exhibition – so every lead must be pursued in the most appropriate way.

There are a few more general points worth making as well.

- *Take a break* You really can't spend more than a couple of hours on a stand without starting to look as tired as you feel. Everyone should have frequent breaks, even if they just spend 15 minutes looking round the other stands (which is well worth doing, to see what your competitors are up to).

- *Keep the stand looking smart* By the third day of the exhibition, most of the stands will have used ashtrays and empty coffee cups lying around them, bits of broken display equipment, empty literature stands or crumpled leaflets. Make sure yours isn't one of them – it's easy to let it happen without noticing.

- *Don't leave anything unattended* From handbags and briefcases to customer records – or even the stand itself at packing up time – err on the side of caution and assume nothing is safe.

PRODUCT DEMONSTRATIONS

Demonstrating a product during a presentation, on an exhibition stand or as part of a sales visit needs a certain finesse. If your product is unusual or new to the customer, the demonstration will be all-important to them, so it must be vital to you as well. Here are the main points you need to consider:

- research the customer's needs and work out which points to make about the product when you demonstrate it – concentrating on the benefits to them, of course

186

- treat the product with respect – you may even be able to capitalise on this; if it's a pioneering, expensive piece of equipment, polish it as you take it out of the packaging

- make sure you've rehearsed the demonstration, double-checked all the working parts and brought spares of anything that could break down or go wrong. And try out the demonstration in the actual location if you possibly can

- you shouldn't talk while you demonstrate the product – tell the customer beforehand what you would like them to notice, demonstrate your product in silence, then reiterate: 'As I mentioned before, you can hear that the whole process is virtually silent . . .'

- get the customer to hold or test out the product

- encourage them to ask you questions about it

- reinforce the demonstration with literature and handouts.

So that's selling. It can be an expensive operation, but if you know what you're doing and target it carefully, every pound you spend will earn itself back with interest.

9

Distribution

Marketing is getting the right goods to the right people in the right place at the right time.

Anon

Distribution is not only a physical operation; it has a marketing dimension as well. It can open up new opportunities and new markets. It can reduce costs, which makes profit increases or price reductions possible, and new initiatives worthwhile.

You have two basic options when it comes to distribution:
1 doing it yourself
2 distributing through someone else – an agent, distributor or retailer.

You have plenty of options when it comes to deciding how to get your goods to the customer; the question is, which approach is the most cost effective?

Distribution can be a horrendously expensive part of your operation, but there is a lot of scope for applying low cost marketing techniques. OK, so you probably won't be able to deliver articulated lorries to Mongolia for nothing, but you can often find that certain approaches will drastically reduce your costs. The key is low cost marketing rule one: *think*.

There are advantages to handling your own distribution, and advantages to reaching your customers via a third party – an agent, wholesaler or retailer. The chief benefits of doing it yourself are:

- you get to keep all the profits
- you (or your own employees) will probably sell your own products or services with more enthusiasm than someone else will.

The main advantages of using a third party are:

- it cuts down on overheads – administration, travel, office space, staffing and so on
- some customers only like to buy from their regular distributor.

If you sell through someone else, they will take a cut of the profit. Your job is to work out how much extra it would cost to do your distribution yourself – take into account your own time, the extra personnel, administration costs of handling all the paperwork yourself, and so on. Then it's a simple matter of comparing the costs.

The other major factor to consider when choosing your distribution channels is your corporate or brand image. Does your distribution outlet give the right impression for the product? If you're selling top quality expensive goods, it might not look too good to use an agent who otherwise sells products known for their 'tatty but cheap' image. When Phileas Fogg crisps and snacks were first launched, they deliberately chose to sell them only through shops with a reputation for quality; you couldn't get them at your local corner shop. Products are judged by the company they keep.

Doing it yourself

About the simplest method of reducing distribution costs is to defray them by delivering other people's (non-competitive) goods at the same time. Suppose you distribute wine to all the top restaurants in the area. Why not find other businesses who deliver cheese, say, or spices to the same restaurants and offer to deliver their products, for a reasonable price?

One of the biggest opportunities for saving money when you're doing your own distribution lies in hitching a lift with someone else who is going the same way. Suppose you want to deliver your garden climbing frames to garden centres at the other end of the country. Look for someone else who is going that way already, and has spare capacity in their vehicle. The key here is to be imaginative; you're not necessarily looking for someone in the same industry as you at all. Probably the easiest way to illustrate this approach is by example, so here are two genuine, and very original, ways to reduce distribution costs.

THE PARIS COACH

In the off-peak season, travel operators continue to run coaches from London to Paris. However, they don't usually manage to fill them completely. Not only does this leave empty seats in the coach, it also means that the luggage compartment is only half full. One enterprising business person in the South of England discovered this and persuaded the coach operator to let them fill the spare space with their cheeses, which they wanted to deliver to Paris once a week (they were clearly very enterprising anyway, managing to sell cheese to the French).

This cost a fraction of what they would have had to spend if they'd transported it to France themselves (they'd organised someone to meet the coach in Paris and unload the cheese), and the coach operator managed to earn some money from what would otherwise have been wasted space.

189

FILLING IN THE GAPS

Another, equally inventive business person wanted to export biscuits to America. He found someone who was going in the same direction, but their lorry was full up – with industrial boilers. Undeterred, he arranged to transport his biscuits *inside* the boilers; he found each boiler could comfortably accommodate 480 tins of biscuits without adding any extra volume to the cargo, and very little extra weight.

Another popular approach to this kind of 'piggyback' distribution is to find businesses that make the same journey as you in the opposite direction. If you want to transport goods from Bristol to Edinburgh, look for someone who delivers from Edinburgh to Bristol and then takes an empty lorry back up to Scotland for the next load. See if your goods can't hitch a lift on the empty truck, for a fraction of the cost of running your own empty lorries home from Edinburgh.

The obvious alternative to this approach is to do the same thing the other way round: *you* operate the fleet, and sell space on the return journey to other businesses who want to move their goods in the opposite direction to you. This approach (both ways round) is becoming increasingly popular for distribution around Europe, with the phasing out of EC haulage restrictions.

OPEN UP THE MARKET

Sometimes distribution can be the key to new markets. You may find someone who does a weekly run to Europe, but doesn't go to Munich, or wherever you want to deliver your goods to. On the other hand, they *do* go to Zurich. Maybe that's just what you needed to make it cost effective to start selling in Switzerland.

190

Once you've discovered that air freight is much cheaper if you send it on standby in the extra space in the hold on scheduled passenger airlines, you may find you can afford to expand into the US or South East Asia. You have no guaranteed time of travel, but you may have a product for which this wouldn't matter.

There are also opportunities if you apply the technique of thinking like a customer. Is your current method of distribution the most helpful for them? It was this line of thinking that first led to dial-a-pizza services, and opened up a huge market in people who didn't want to go out for a take-away, but would happily order one if they didn't have to move from their chair.

Agents, distributors and retailers

Many people assume that it's better to sell direct and avoid paying someone else a share of the profit, but this is often a false economy. You might be able to visit 20 customers a week. Or you could visit one distributor and leave yourself 19 free appointments to go and look for new outlets, while the distributor looks after your first 20 customers.

What's more, you only have to worry about 1 invoice – the distributor has to deal with the other 20. That's more administration time freed up to spend planning or selling instead of poring over paperwork.

It makes a lot of difference what your product is, how expensive it is to distribute, and what your administration costs are. Sometimes it pays to handle your own distribution. But if you decide to reach your customers through someone else, you have five main options:

1 agents
2 distributors/wholesalers
3 retailers
4 home distributors
5 selling to syndicates.

One of the most important things to remember when you use this kind of distribution is that someone else is dealing with your customers for you. And you want to be sure that they treat them as well as you would yourself. So work hard to motivate and enthuse them. Get them interested in pushing your product. Tell them what you're planning. Thank them, congratulate them, invite them to your product launches or Christmas party. And ask their advice – they're your best source of low cost market research information. So keep closely in touch, and follow low cost marketing rule two: *talk*.

AGENTS

An agent sells your product on your behalf, but you don't actually employ them. You invoice the customer direct, and pay the agent a commission: usually between 7.5 and 15%.

You and your agents need to agree (preferably in a written contract) not to compete with each other. In other words, they should not be selling any of your competitors' products, and you shouldn't try to sell direct to the same customers as them.

To find an agent, either ask your retailers for recommendations, put an advertisement in the trade press or contact one of the two national organisations for agents: the British Agents Register or the Manufacturers' Agents Association (see Useful Addresses at the end of this book).

DISTRIBUTORS/WHOLESALERS

Distributors are different from agents. They are customers – big customers usually – and should be treated accordingly. They buy direct from you and add on a mark-up; probably between 30 and 100%. This can be a very low cost way to distribute as you have only a few, large customers, which keeps your overheads very low. It's also better for your cash flow than waiting for the customer's money to come back from agents. However, the fewer distributors you use, the more vulnerable you are if they change policy, decide not to stock that line any more, or go bust.

If you export, this is often a good way to sell your product overseas. It can also be a good idea to set up a mutual distribution deal or partnership with a foreign company. For example, if you find a business in Italy that manufactures ornate, carved wooden garden arches, they might distribute Arabesque in Italy while you distribute their products in the UK. You each have a ready-made channel to your own country's garden centres and landscape designers. The Business Co-operative Network or BC-Net (your local office of the Department of Trade and Industry (DTI) will put you in touch) helps businesses to find European partners, as do many local enterprise agencies.

RETAILERS

The principles for selling to retailers are essentially the same as for selling to distributors and wholesalers; it is simply the outlet that is different. Retailers sell directly over the counter, rather than selling on to other outlets or selling by phone or face-to-face appointments.

You can put a higher price on your product than you would for a wholesaler because it isn't going to be sold on to another outlet with another mark-up to add on. On the other hand, one wholesaler may deal with dozens of retailers, and it will cost you more to reach them all individually than to reach them in a group via the wholesaler.

HOME DISTRIBUTORS

This is how Tupperware started selling – through a 'party plan' set-up. Self employed organisers arrange parties in private houses at which they sell products to the owner of the house and their invited friends. You sell to the organiser at a discount and they add on a mark-up.

You can set up your own party plan operation, but it will only be successful if you are prepared to put in a lot of time organising and motivating the planners, or agents – being self employed, many of them only arrange parties when they want to earn a bit of money, which may not be as often as you want to make a sale. If you're going into this form of distribution for the first time, it's probably better to add your product to the portfolio of established party planners (they're in *Yellow Pages* under Party planners), at least to start with.

193

Obviously this kind of distribution lends itself to certain products. Apart from Tupperware, cosmetics and lingerie do notoriously well. It stands to reason that people would rather buy a pound of carrots in the shops on the day they want them, but the products that sell well through party plan are those that:

- people want to test or try on before they buy them
- people are more likely to buy with friends around them encouraging them
- some people might feel uncomfortable or embarrassed about buying publicly in a shop.

SELLING TO SYNDICATES

If you can, it may be worth inviting groups of customers to club together and buy in syndicate. You can offer them the enticement of a lower price for doing so, while you have the advantage of a guaranteed minimum order. One fisherman on the south coast of England found a group of customers in Hampstead, London, that was willing to take a fixed, minimum order if he would drive his catch straight up to London first thing in the morning. He knew he could do enough business to make it worthwhile, and they got their fish fresher than anyone else in the neighbourhood.

10

Expanding the market

*In truth, I believe there is no such thing as a growth industry.
There are only companies organised and operated to create and
capitalise on growth opportunities. Industries that assume
themselves to be riding some automatic growth escalator
invariably descend into stagnation.*

Theodore Levitt

**If you have lots of money to spare, you can expand your business by
buying up other successful companies. But if you haven't got those
kinds of funds, you'll have to find other ways of growing. Actually,
even if you had the money, these ways would usually be more cost
effective.**

**The best way to expand your business is with a two-pronged attack, the
two prongs being:**

1 find new customers for your products and services
2 find new products and services for your customers.

**In this chapter, we'll have a look at how to put both these approaches into
practice.**

New customers for your products

You should find it easy to build up a list of new leads and contacts
to pursue once you get started. This isn't something to do on a
Friday afternoon when you've run out of other jobs for the
moment. This should be a constant exercise, with lists of new
contacts to follow up all the time – you need never be at a loose end
on a Friday afternoon again. Here are some of the most common
ways to build up a new contact list.

- *Ask customers for referrals* If your customers like your product, they will be happy to refer you to other possible customers. If they are business customers, they may put you on to other buyers in their own organisation or contacts in other companies.

- Trawl the press for details of new businesses in the area, companies with new tenders and contracts, or new products in your industry – anything that suggests they have the makings of a new customer.

- *Business directories and trade associations* The sources we looked at in Chapter 2 should give you new leads.

- *Ask for details with every enquiry* Ask for names and addresses from everyone who contacts you to ask for a brochure or comes up to your stand at a trade show.

- *Direct response advertising* Every time you advertise in the paper or by direct mail, you should ask people to respond – call for a quote, return the coupon or whatever. All these contacts need to be followed up so you can convert them into customers.

- *Buying mailing lists* We looked at this in Chapter 7; it can be an excellent way of reaching new prospects.

- *Market the product differently* You may be able to adapt your core product so that it appeals to a different customer group, then advertise it to this new group. 3M's basic business is coating tape – Scotch tape is the most famous of their products – but they've always looked for new markets for coated tape. They coat audio and video tape, they sell masking tape to painters, surgical tape to hospitals, and Post-it notes to offices. In fact, they now have more products than employees.

- *Change the price* A really big price reduction can lead to a massive volume increase if it takes you into a new market (although this approach must be used very wisely, as we saw in Chapter 3). The calculator was a professional and commercial instrument until Clive Sinclair dropped the price so dramatically it became standard equipment for every schoolchild. Encyclopedias were only for libraries, universities and schools until Britannica had the inspiration to sell them door-to-door on hire purchase.

Of course, as we saw in Chapter 7, a huge list of people to mail is very expensive to run, so you need to prioritise your new contacts. It's impossible to make hard and fast rules as every business differs, but in general:

- people who have approached you are likely to be the most promising
- names you have acquired through third-party contacts, such as referrals, should be the next most likely to yield results
- names you have found in the papers, or acquired from mailing lists, have the lowest yield, though they may still be well worth the effort of contacting. Obviously there are exceptions to this lower response rate – if the mailing list is very well targeted, it will do better; if the new local company in the paper is in one of the key industries you supply, you have a greater chance. Your research should give you these kinds of pointers for prioritising – it may tell you that you sell more to production managers than to buyers, for example, so you could send out a selective mailshot to production managers only.

197

You can break down your list into sections according to location, likely level of interest, range or product they are most likely to buy or whatever suits your business. Then you can contact selected groups – for example, you could invite only the names in the Midlands to visit your exhibition stand at the NEC in Birmingham, or send your garden fencing catalogue to one group and the one of free-standing frames to a different group. Of course, you'd follow up any serious enquiry with the other brochure as well, but it saves the cost of printing one of each for everyone before you know how likely they are to buy.

As we saw in Chapter 7, you'll need to clean your list as often as possible – every person or business on it who has moved house or changed job, or is never going to buy from you, is another wasted stamp, envelope, brochure and all the rest of it. A lot of companies automatically remove everyone from their regular list who hasn't made a purchase in, say, two years (the time span for some products will be very different, of course). You could mail all these people one last time to let them know that you are going to remove them from your list unless they return the coupon. This can trigger a good response, and the people who bother to reply should be useful contacts.

EXPORTING

If you're just starting to export, there are a few tips it may help you to know about:

- The DTI Overseas Trade Services (which you can contact through your regional branch of the DTI) offers a lot of opportunities, many of them free or even sponsored, for finding customers abroad. They can give financial support for attending trade fairs, help you with press releases and publicity overseas, and run an export marketing research scheme. They also hold a database of sales leads around the world from which they can select any opportunities in your industry, and they'll give you help with paperwork and legal advice. You'll find that many local enterprise agencies offer a lot of these services as well.

- Don't assume that just because your product or service sells in the UK, it will necessarily sell abroad. Even apparently similar cultures can have totally different tastes. For example, the Germans generally buy fast-spin washing machines, but the Italians prefer to slow-spin their clothes, while the French like top-loaders. So make sure you research your target market thoroughly, following the guidelines in Chapter 2, of course.

- You may well find it easier to start out exporting to countries that speak English – if your product allows it. It makes it far easier to produce written material, from packaging and instruction booklets to advertisements and sales literature, and to chase up leads yourself. Mind you, if you are fluent in any other languages, that could well give you a lead over all your British competitors.

- One of the easiest forms of exporting, from an administrative point of view, is selling to export buyers. These organisations (listed in the *Directory of Export Buyers*, which you will find in larger libraries) are agents for foreign companies; they select

198

and buy British goods on their behalf. Selling to them can take a while, as the buyers they act for may not visit the UK to see their samples for months at a time, but it is often very worthwhile.

■ If you use an overseas agent or distributor (DTI Overseas Trade Services can help you find them) they will effectively bring a ready-made customer list with them, and they will take on the task of expanding this list.

■ We looked at the possibility of finding overseas partners in Chapter 9, and if you do this, it will give you instant access to their customers and leads.

New products for your customers

The continuous research we looked at in Chapter 2 should keep you well informed about any changes in your customers' preferences or your industry's trends. You should always be on the lookout for new products you can sell to your existing cus-tomers. This doesn't only mean developing more ideas, but also finding add-on products that would appeal to the same market – like Mars bringing out the Mars ice-cream bar. For example, Arabesque might find that a lot of customers would buy fencing in four-foot lengths or want arches to fit into a run of fencing. But why not also think about a totally different product – and sell roses and clematis as well?

Here are a few more examples of associated products:

■ nursery rhyme books in children's shoe departments

■ orange juice, cakes, butter and eggs on the milk round

■ cookery books in supermarkets

■ corkscrews, wine glasses, labels, even olive oil with mail-order wine.

KEEPING CUSTOMER RECORDS

Clearly you will need to record as much information as you can in order to know how your customers respond to your products, what they buy and when, and what new products they might be interested in. These records are one of your most valuable research sources, as we saw in Chapter 2. You will probably keep these records on computer, in which case make sure you comply with the Data Protection Act. You should record the following information for each customer:

1 address, phone and fax numbers, and name of company for business customers
2 name of customer, or names and job titles of the main contacts at a business address
3 type of business
4 a record of their transactions with you:
   - what they bought
   - when they bought it
   - what quantity they bought
5 a history of payments, payment times and customer's credit rating
6 a record of any visits to the customer, or sales phone calls
7 a record of any problems or complaints, including the relevant dates, and how they were resolved.

So in order to keep growing and expanding your market, without investing money in it that you haven't got, you need to be continuously on the lookout for new customers, and new products and services. And as long as you remember to practise the four rules of low cost marketing – think, talk, do it yourself, and keep it simple – there'll be no stopping you.

Useful addresses

■

British Agents Register
24 Mount Parade, Harrogate, North Yorkshire HG1 1BP
0423 560608

Business in the Community
8 Stratton Street, London W1X 5FD
071 629 1600

Central Statistical Office
Information Services Department, Government Buildings, Great
George Street, London SW1P 3AQ
071 270 6364

Companies House
55 City Road, London EC1Y 1BB
071 253 9393

or

Crown Way, Cardiff CF4 3UZ
0222 388588

The Data Protection Registrar
Springfield House, Water Lane, Wilmslow, Cheshire SK9 5AX

Direct Marketing Association (UK) Ltd
Haymarket House, 1 Oxendon Street, London SW1Y 4EE
071 321 2525

Exhibition Bulletin
272 Kirkdale, London SE26 4RZ
081 778 2288

Manufacturers' Agents Association
1 Somers Road, Reigate, Surrey RH2 9DU
0737 241025

Market Research Society
15 North Burgh Street, London EC1V 0AH
071 490 4911

Science Reference Library
25 Southampton Buildings, Chancery Lane, London WC2A 1AW
071 636 1544

***Yellow Pages* Business Database**
8 Waterside Drive, Langley, Slough SL3 6EZ
081 567 7300

Index

■

205